W9-BGM-474

The Complete Book of

Woodburning
Stoves

The Complete Book of
Woodburning Stoves

David Ivins

DRAKE PUBLISHERS INC.
NEW YORK · LONDON

Published in 1978 by
Drake Publishers, Inc.
801 Second Avenue
New York, N.Y. 10017

Library of Congress Cataloging in Publication Data

Ivins, David, 1928-
The complete book of woodburning stoves.

Bibliography: p.
Includes index.
1. Stoves, Wood.   I. Title.
TH7438.I94   643'.1   78-56961
ISBN 0-8473-1760-9

Printed in the United States of America

Design: Harold Franklin

Contents

The Complete Book of
Woodburning
Stoves

Chapter 1

The
Wood Fuel
Renaissance

Since the onset of the energy crisis, Americans have been seeking methods of saving fuel—as well as money—and getting some personal satisfaction out of our tradition of "beating the system." The greatest challenge they face is in their money-saving attempts to cut fuel bills at home.

The cost of heating oil continues to rise, and we have responded by lowering our thermostats and spending millions of dollars on insulating materials and new or better storm windows. But we can lower those thermostats only so much, and the costs of insulating materials and storm windows have also skyrocketed. The supply of insulation of various types hasn't been able to keep up with demand.

An increasing number of American homeowners, slowly at first but now at an accelerating rate, have rediscovered what was once the sole source of heat for eons: the forests, trees, *wood*, our oldest fuel.

Mankind's discovery of fire is at least as important as his discovery—or invention—of such modern technological miracles as the internal-combustion engine, the telephone, and the cathode ray tube that gave us television.

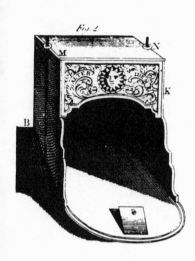

Benjamin Franklin's drawings for his Pennsylvanian Fire-place. Fig. 2 (above) is the stove body; 1 (below) is the stove floor; iii (opposite page) is a side panel with grooves for IV (middle plates with air channels). The broken lines and arrows denote the flow of heated air. V is the decorated front plate. Viii is the draft control shutter.

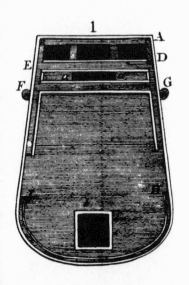

Fire not only kept primitive man warm in his cave. It also encouraged him to bring home the animals that he hunted so that his mate could cook the meat (since it tasted better that way) instead of consuming it raw at the site of the kill and just carrying home leftovers to be tossed to his mate and offspring. Thus fire became something of a socializing influence and helped to build stronger family ties and a sense of tribal community. Fire also gave primitive man light, which made nighttime less fearful. His cave became a place to communicate with story-telling and drawings that still exist on cave walls today.

Fire kept at bay the beasts who saw *homo sapiens*, the relatively weak, defenseless two-legged creature, as nothing more than an easily obtainable meal. Fire deterred even the hungriest predatory animal.

As man learned to build shelters of stone, wood, adobe, and even ice blocks, the location of the wood fire was always one of his main considerations, whether for cooking in warm climates or for life-sustaining warmth in cold climates.

As his shelters became more sophisticated, man's devices for cooking and keeping warm became more ingenious and efficient. From the cave with its small fire (and perhaps a natural fissure in the roof to act as a chimney) evolved everything from the Eskimo's igloo to the Empire State Building with many stops in between and beyond. They all are heated by fire in one way or another.

By medieval times a device called a fireplace had evolved, and with it the lowly peasant was one-up on his lord and master. The small fireplace in the peasant's wood-and-mud hut kept him and his family warmer than did the fireplaces in the nobleman's damp, drafty stone castle. The nobles had to sacrifice a certain amount of comfort for prestige and the safety of stone walls and high ground where the winds took much of the fire's heat up through the chimney.

Eventually, of course, the noblemen abandoned their castles when the style of warfare changed—the peasants were "drafted" and the high-born stayed home. They built even more luxurious dwellings that were capable of being heated more easily due to advances in what might be called "fireplace technology," but a fireplace was still just a fireplace and left much to be desired. It was—and still is—comparatively inefficient in providing usable heat. Fireplaces burn wood quickly while extracting from it only ten to twenty percent of its heat-giving energy. But scientists and craftsmen were continually on the job all over the world.

In America Benjamin Franklin is generally credited with inventing the stove which he called the "Pennsylvanian Fire-place." Franklin designed this prototype of the American woodburning stove because of a Colonial-era energy crisis in Philadelphia. Inefficient fireplaces ate wood the way a 1960s Cadillac ate gasoline. The forests outside Philadelphia and the other cities of the mid- to late 1700s were being depleted. Americans knew nothing about the science of forestry. The tree supply looked infinite to them.

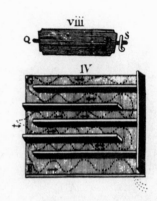

The ingenious Ben Franklin came to the rescue. His Pennsylvanian Fire-place was made of cast iron, its components bolted together, and the spaces between them sealed. In effect it was an open-front stove fitted into a fireplace that had been bricked up except for a passageway that led from the stove to the floor beneath the fireplace and finally to the chimney. In this way the smoke was vented.

To allow the wood to burn more slowly than was possible in an open fireplace, Franklin equipped his invention with a damper which regulated the flow of air to the flames. About halfway back in the development of the Pennsylvanian there were upright metal plates which formed baffles. The gases formed by the burning wood were themselves burned as fuel. The baffles also kept the heat in the stove for a period of time, allowing it to radiate into the room. These sophisticated innovations are still used today in modified form in even the most advanced woodburning stoves.

Over the next quarter-century, the Franklin fireplace (or Franklin stove, as it was being called) was manufactured by various craftsmen in foundries throughout the American Colonies. Franklin never patented his device; he believed that such things should benefit everyone without restriction. There might have been more than personal philosophy behind this belief since there are historians who say his Pennsylvanian Fire-place used concepts that had not originated with Franklin or were, at best, variations on the ideas of others.

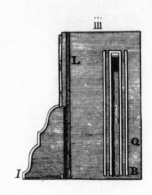

Franklin did become annoyed at a number of so-called improvements on his invention. The only actual improvement seems to be the discovery that the Franklin fireplace worked even better outside the fireplace enclosure, free-standing, with a length of metal pipe leading from the stove to the chimney.

In 1816 the "Franklin stove" was patented. The name is still used today for a variety of stoves that operate on principles of Franklin's Pennsylvanian Fireplace. A few of them are still designed to fit inside a fireplace enclosure.

When the first settlers arrived in the New World from Europe, most of the Northeast was densely forested with wood for homes, barns, farm tools, wagons, furniture—and heat. The supply of wood fuel looked inexhaustible to the men and women who began clearing the land to build homesteads and villages. Today, despite continuing abuse of our forests—clear-cutting, failure to replant trees, waste on an incredible scale—America still has close to seventy-five percent of the forest land that existed two hundred years ago. This forest treasure (about 750 million acres) will remain abundant with wise management and represents a renewable source of fuel for our homes. Knowledgeable Americans are taking advantage of that fact.

In Vermont, one of the New England states known for long, cold winters, eighty percent of the homes relied on No. 2 fuel oil for heat in 1970. By 1976 less than seventy percent of the Vermont homes were being heated solely by No. 2 heating oil. In that same period, the percentage of homes relying on wood alone as heating fuel rose from barely one percent to more than seven percent.

In Maine, where seventy-five percent of the land area is still forest, Governor James Longley said that perhaps seventy-five percent of the state's home-owners were using wood stoves for heat at least part of the winter, thus conserving high-priced oil by using wood as an auxiliary fuel either in old stoves they had reactivated after years of disuse, or in newly purchased stoves.

About eighty percent of the land area in New England is forested. Although much of that land is owned by lumber and paper companies, enough is privately held so that homeowners can obtain wood from their own land, free, for use as fuel. Obviously many of them are doing so.

In all states where the winters are long and harsh, wood heat is making a comeback. Even commercial enterprises are experimenting with wood. In Vermont, Burlington Electric recently converted one of its three power turbines to burn what is known as "cull wood"—otherwise useless twigs, branches, roots, and sawdust. And although the company says it is usually necessary to burn natural gas with the wood to reach a high

The Acme *Oak Heater*, an ornate parlor stove from the Sears, Roebuck and Co. catalog of 1911. Decorations were silver nickel-plated. Price for the largest model: $12.10. *Photo courtesy of Sears, Roebuck and Co.*

Also from the 1911 Sears, Roebuck and Co. catalog, the Acme *Wildwood* and Wehrle No. 193 airtights. *Photo courtesy of Sears, Roebuck and Co.*

temperature, the conversion is still a worthwhile experiment and is being continued.

The Weyerhaueser Lumber Company in Washington has the best of all possible worlds: it is able to generate fifty percent of its own power requirements by burning the mountains of wood scraps that accumulate through timber cutting.

Besides being a renewable resource, wood, when burned as fuel, does far less damage to our environment than do mining for coal and drilling for oil. The smoke from burning wood is not considered to be air pollution. Another beneficial factor in the use of wood for fuel is that wood can be cut and used on the spot without having to be transported by truck or ship to the consumer. Transportation adds dollars to every ton of coal and every gallon of oil, and the consumer pays the price. All that is needed to "process" wood is a brief period of time for it to dry.

Oil fields and refineries, access roads, huge trucks, oil tankers and their attendant disastrous oil spills in oceans and inland waterways, strip mining and deep mining for coal and their destruction of millions of acres of land—all contribute to the degradation of our natural environment in one way or another. And the amount of energy to run the refineries, heavy mining equipment, trucks, oil tankers, and so on is enormous and part of the cycle of environmental damage and a waste of non-renewable resources that may be irreversible.

Wood is non-polluting and requires much less human and mechanical energy to produce and distribute. The smoke produced by burning wood is merely the result of a speeding-up of the natural decaying process of wood. It is basically composed of the same chemicals.

Wood is a tough cellulose material, so tough that paper can be recycled numerous times. So the natural decomposition of a log or fallen tree takes many years. Only fire accelerates that process, and in that process, heat is produced with no pollutants.

In contrast, when fossil fuel (oil and coal) is burned, we get not only heat but such pollutants as sulphur dioxide which is harmful to man and the natural environment. It is sulphur dioxide that causes buildings and stone statues to discolor and eventually crumble. You can imagine what such a chemical does to our lungs and other organs and cells.

To advocate even a gradual return to the exclusive use of wood as fuel would be absurd for obvious reasons, but on a modest scale, as is happening now, wood can be a useful supplement to our customary fuels: oil, coal, natural gas, and electricity.

This rediscovery of wood as fuel has taken wood stove manufacturing and retailing—a once steady but

The Wehrle No. 20, from the 1911 Sears, Roebuck and Co. catalog, was "A good looker, a good cooker, a good baker, economical and durable." *Photo courtesy of Sears, Roebuck and Co.*

limited industry—and suddenly turned it into a booming field comparable to such recreational growth industries as skiing, tennis, and, most recently, running. According to estimates, 500,000 woodburning stoves were sold in this country in 1977—about $150 million worth. The major manufacturers say their orders are backed up for months. Few of the manufacturers, importers, distributors, and retailers were prepared for the boom, but none are complaining about their sudden prosperity.

In Vermont, one state where such data is available, another group of people involved with the "wood fuel renaissance" are prospering: woodsmen and wood dealers. The wood fuel business is growing with the speed of a fast-food chain. And the entrepreneurs of that ancient business are cashing in on a combination of Yankee ingenuity and modern marketing techniques.

Foresters are experimenting with "whole-tree har-

The Wehrle No. 66, from the 1911 Sears, Roebuck and Co. catalog, had a glass window in the oven door so you could "Watch the progress of baking...." *Photo courtesy of Sears, Roebuck and Co.*

vesting" equipment which, as the term implies, takes everything the tree has to offer for possible use, even the sawdust. Other logging equipment includes a newly invented machine capable of cutting an entire tree into lengths of the right size for a stove and splitting the logs to desired thicknesses. Still another device, used in Canada but not yet in this country, bundles logs into cords on pallets to be loaded onto trucks, shipped to dealers, and stored for seasoning—all quickly, easily, and with little wasted space.

Wood is being marketed differently in Vermont, too. Supermarkets now offer plastic bags of wood chips for use as kindling, and smaller stores are offering logs "six-pack"-style, in cardboard cartons with carrying handles. The price, however, is about $2.75 per pack. For the unknowledgeable, now-and-then wood burner, that amounts to $600 per cord of wood. That's a ripoff. In Vermont a cord sells for $50 to $100, depending on the area.

The established wood dealers have high hopes for the continuing prosperity of their businesses without ripping anyone off. Previously they sold wood only to local people. Now many of them see markets for cordwood as far away as Boston and New York City where higher prices can be charged because of the natural law of supply and demand. A cord of wood sells for $100 to $125 in those cities, and the buyer will be getting a good deal since fuel oil is higher priced there than in rural areas.

Oil dealers in Vermont last winter were in trouble because of the increasing reliance on wood fuel. With an estimated fifty percent of Vermont homeowners using wood for heat at least part of the time, many fuel oil dealers were suffering from what is politely called a "cash-flow problem." They weren't able to pay their bills on time, and they were having trouble getting credit.

A state oil industry spokesman said that in 1974, there were 190 fuel oil dealers in Vermont. In the winter of 1977-78, there were only about 120 dealers. The spokesman estimated that by the end of 1978, there might be fewer than 100.

Not all of this was caused by the increase in wood burning, of course, since Vermonters have been installing insulation in their homes and conserving

The *Olympic* Franklin stove, vented through the existing fireplace, with doors open for viewing the fire. *Photo courtesy of Sears, Roebuck and Co.*

A parlor stove by Washington Stove Works. Castings are made from original hand-carved patterns. Nickel-plated decorations are available as options. *Photo courtesy of Washington Stove Works.*

heating oil, but wood burning has certainly contributed to the decline of fuel oil sales and thus to the failure of a number of oil businesses.

At this stage of the wood fuel renaissance, it is obviously the individual American, beset by rising fuel costs and seemingly ever colder winters, who benefits most by the return of the woodburning stove. Before we rush out to buy a woodburner or two, there are many things to consider.

Whether he lives in the suburbs or a rural area, the homeowner is accustomed to the reliability and ease of operation of that quiet, unobtrusive oil or gas furnace or electric heater in the cellar. An oil burner does most of the work through the magic of modern technology. You set the room thermostats, and that's about it for the winter—if it's a normal winter, the heater doesn't break down, and there isn't a fuel shortage or a strike by the oil delivery men.

Wood stoves must be tended to one extent or another: you fuel the stove, check it, clean it. As yet, wood stove technology hasn't devised an automated method of picking up a chunk of wood, opening the stove door, and tossing the log onto the fire.

You get the idea. But the money you save with a wood burning stove is more than worth such minor physical effort. Let's take a look at the economics of heating with wood, either as a home's sole source of fuel or as a money-saving back-up system.

Don't expect to begin saving big money the first winter. You may, depending on individual circumstances, but don't count on it. Consider the purchase of a woodburning stove, its installation, the cost of a cord or two of wood, and possible modifications or repairs to your chimney as an investment which may take a winter or two to pay off—but pay off it will.

Estimating exactly how much money you will save over a winter is all but impossible. The prices of heating fuels and electrical power (whichever you use) and the prices of cord wood vary from one area of the country to another. In addition, the amount of wood you need depends on the number of rooms you want to heat, which determines the size and type of stove you need, which in turn determines its price. But your investment will pay off not only in bankable dollars but in a certain peace of mind in knowing that whatever happens—a fuel shortage, oil burner breakdown during 10-degree weather, power failure, or strike—you and your family will have at least one warm room in the house. That alone is worth your investment and work. Ask anyone who went for days or weeks without heat and was perhaps forced to live in an armory or other makeshift shelter, or at a hotel or motel (think of that expense), or with relatives in another state or city.

A rough estimate of the comparative cost of wood versus coal, oil, and electricity can be made when you know that a cord of fuel wood will provide about the same amount of heat as approximately 200 gallons of No. 2 fuel oil, a ton of coal, or 4,000 kwh of electricity. (The heat-giving qualities of various types of wood are discussed in Chapter 5.) If you've kept your fuel bills over the years, you'll be able to get a rough idea as to how much money you can save over a winter by utilizing wood as fuel.

Besides the cost of the stove and the wood to feed it, you'll also have to pay certain labor and material costs for locating the chimney flues in the room or rooms where you plan to install a stove. In a newer home it will be necessary to break through a wall to the chimney flue and make a hole for a six- or eight-inch stovepipe (a procedure covered in Chapter 3). Your chimney flue may need to be cleaned (this is a good thing to do anyway).

If you own an older home, you may discover a couple of bricked-up fireplaces that you never knew about because they'd been plastered over and then covered with layers of paint and wallpaper. (So that's what that bulge in the wall is!) This is a lucky find, since you can enjoy the pleasure of an old-time fireplace and the warmth of a stove by venting the stove through the fireplace flue. First, of course, you'll have to uncover the fireplace, but that's a job you and the family can do with a minimum of time and expense.

A stove in a summer home, cabin, or garage-workshop is ideal for cooking and for chilly or rainy evenings in the spring or summer.

It is possible to install a woodburning stove in whatever type of dwelling you own. The work involved in preparation and installation will save you money in the long run.

Another point to keep in mind: As part of President Carter's energy bill, there will be a tax credit of twenty percent of the cost of installation, up to a maximum of $400, for homeowners who install a woodburning stove. Now if Congress ever gets around to passing the bill . . .

This Franklin stove by Birmingham Stove & Range Co. has tempered glass door panels. *Photo courtesy of Birmingham Stove & Range Co.*

Chapter 2

Buying
the Right Stove

You've decided to join the wood fuel renaissance. No, you're not about to scrap your central-heating system and install two or three wood stoves in the house. That would be impractical and expensive, and there are too many unknown factors involved, but a wood stove is perfect to heat the living room during the evenings and on weekends since that's where most of the family congregates to watch TV, listen to records, or just "hang out." The other rooms are practically unused then, so you can turn down their thermostats and watch your fuel bills drop proportionately.

Consider this stove-buying venture an experiment. If you decide later on that it's worthwhile (which it may well be, with continually rising fuel prices, colder winters, and possible oil shortages) you may want to go all-out, buy a stove or two, and heat the entire house with wood fuel. You might even convert your present furnace to a wood-burner (yes, there are woodburning furnaces for central heating). Right now, one stove for the living room is all you want, but before you head for the nearest stove dealer or mail your check for that

Parlor Stove

Kitchen Stove

Box Stove

Potbelly Stove

Fireplace Stove

TYPES OF STOVES

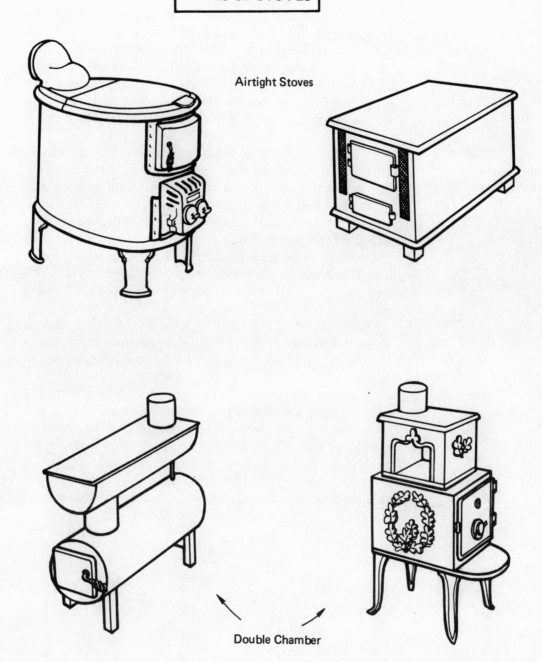

Airtight Stoves

Double Chamber

Though designs vary, these are typical stoves. *Illustration by S. Mackay, courtesy of Northeast Regional Agricultural Engineering Service.*

great-looking stove you saw in a catalog, you've got some homework to do.

Choosing the right stove for your purposes isn't as complex as, say, buying a separate-component stereo system, a 35mm single lens reflex camera, or a new car, where there are seemingly countless brands, models, sizes, and types to consider, but it comes close. Since most Americans are unfamiliar with woodburning stoves, making a choice can be that much more difficult.

Most of us have at least heard about wood stoves during the last couple of years. Few of us, unless we live in a rural area, know much about how they actually work. Most people assume you crumple up a few sheets of paper, stuff them into the stove, add kindling, and light the paper. Once the kindling is burning well, you toss in some heavier sticks of wood or a couple of logs. The fire gets hotter and you're warm. When the logs have burned down in a couple of hours, you add more, and so on.

Basically that's how it works. But there is much more to the woodburning stove, especially now that it has been touched by new ideas and modern technology.

Many of the best stoves today are called *airtights* because they are literally airtight. They allow wood to burn slowly and steadily in a controlled fire that is almost as free of fluctuating temperatures as is an oil heater or electric heater, and they can burn for up to fourteen hours without refueling.

The airtight stoves have inner baffles to control the

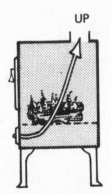

UP

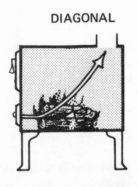

DIAGONAL

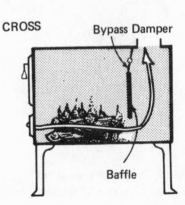

CROSS

Bypass Damper

Baffle

flow of unburned gases (volatiles) inside the stove. These volatiles are redirected so they pass over the flames and are themselves burned, thus increasing the amount of radiated heat instead of allowing it to escape through the chimney.

Other stoves have a "downdraft" system which serves the same purpose as a baffle: to burn the gases as completely as possible and generate more usable heat.

A number of stoves have various accessories to increase the amount of radiated heat or direct it to where it is needed. Much depends on how the owner uses his stove—properly or improperly—just as in the use of a

DRAFT CONFIGURATIONS

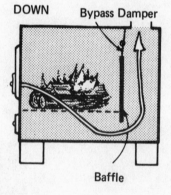

Baffles are designed to increase the length of the flame path.

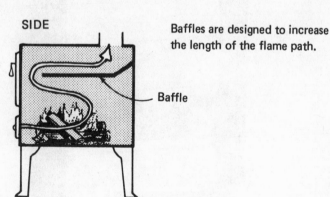

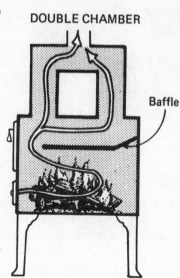

A stove's draft system is one of the crucial factors that determines its efficiency. *Illustration by S. Mackay, courtesy of Northeast Regional Agricultural Engineering Service.*

car. Abuse a car and it runs poorly; "baby" it and it runs well.

Your choice of a stove depends on several factors, most of them unfamiliar except the amount of money you want to spend, (a consideration in buying anything). The next important factor to consider is the amount of space available in the room you want to heat. If you've been living in your home for many years you may have a rough idea of its dimensions. But any gambler would bet his entire bank account that you—and most homeowners—have no idea how many cubic feet there are in your living room. That is the most important factor in determining the size of the stove you need, and in large part, the size determines the price of the stove.

Measure the size of your living room in cubic feet. The formula is length multiplied by width, multiplied

Made in Austria, the Tirolia 120-10 is an airtight of steel and cast iron with a porcelain enamel finish. The manufacturer says it "Burns anything — wood, coal, scraps." *Photo courtesy of "Old Country" Appliances.*

The Jøtul No. 118 airtight. The ornamental bas-relief is by Norwegian artist Ørnulf Bast. The inscription reads: "I built me a flame late one night. When day is done God will my flame never dies out." *Photo courtesy of Kristia Associates, exclusive importers of Jøtul stoves, Portland, Maine 04104.*

by height (in case you've forgotten your grade-school mathematics).

Let's say your living room is 28 feet long by 20 feet wide with an 8-foot ceiling. That works out to 4,480 cubic feet to be heated. Round that off to 4,500, and you are on target—so far.

There are other factors to consider:

• Is there a lot of furniture in the room—chairs, sofa, bookcases, and such? A stove's ability to heat is determined not only by a room's volume but also by its surface area; that includes the objects in the room.

• Are there such things as alcoves, a bay window, an

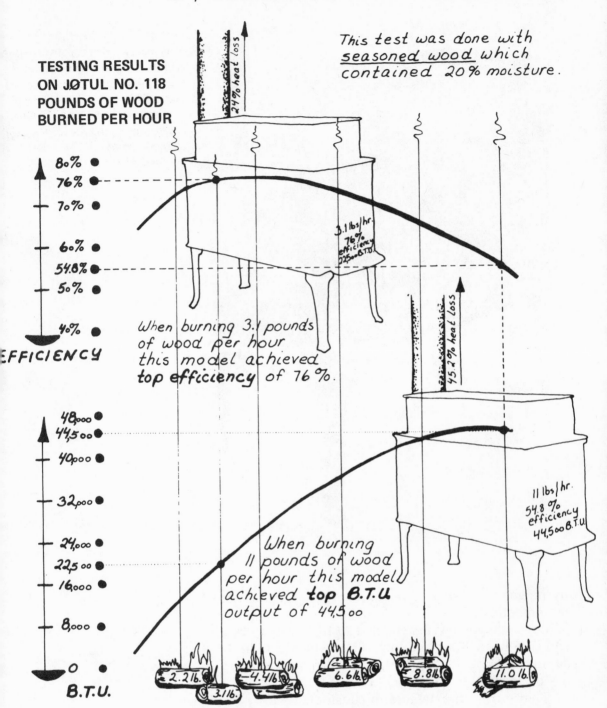

TESTING RESULTS ON JØTUL NO. 118 POUNDS OF WOOD BURNED PER HOUR

This test was done with seasoned wood which contained 20% moisture.

24% heat loss

80%
76%
70%
60%
54.8%
50%
40%

EFFICIENCY

3.1 lbs/hr.
76%
efficiency
22,500 B.T.U.

When burning 3.1 pounds of wood per hour this model achieved **top efficiency** of 76%.

45.2% heat loss

48,000
44,500
40,000
32,000
24,000
22,500
16,000
8,000
0

B.T.U.

11 lbs/hr.
54.8% efficiency
44,500 B.T.U.

When burning 11 pounds of wood per hour this model achieved **top B.T.U** output of 44,500

2.2 lb.
3.1 lb.
4.4 lb.
6.6 lb.
8.8 lb.
11.0 lb.

Efficiency tests were conducted by the Jøtul testing laboratories. The Jøtul No. 118 achieved 76% efficiency. *Diagram courtesy of Kristia Associates, exclusive importers of Jøtul stoves, Portland, Maine 04104.*

archway leading to a dining room, or another type of doorway that cannot be closed off? If so, you'll have to include that area in your calculations because heat will be drawn there.

• Are there unusually large windows, or more windows than are normally found in a room of comparable size?

The Jøtul No. 606's arch design provides a larger area for heat radiation. The ornamental bas-relief is by Ørnulf Bast. *Photo courtesy of Kristia Associates, exclusive importers of Jøtul stoves, Portland, Maine 04104.*

TESTING RESULTS ON JØTUL NO. 606 POUNDS OF WOOD BURNED PER HOUR

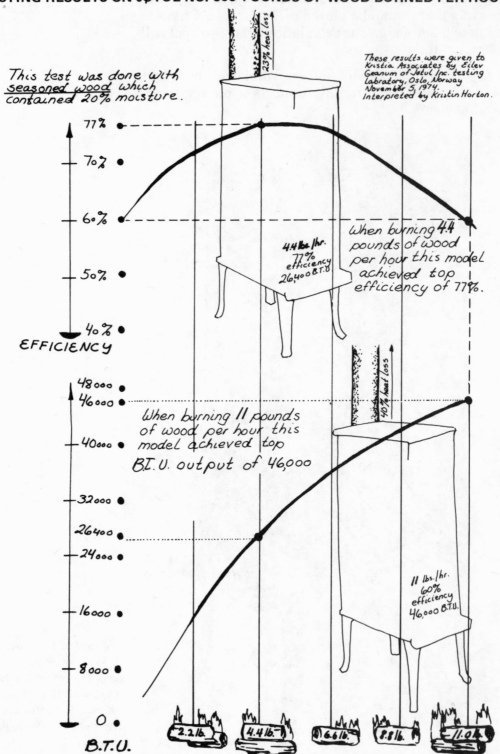

This test was done with seasoned wood which contained 20% moisture.

These results were given to Kristia Associates by Eiler Granum of Jøtul Inc. testing labratory, Oslo, Norway November 5, 1974. Interpreted by Kristin Horton.

23% heat loss

77%

70%

60%

50%

40%

EFFICIENCY

4.4 lbs./hr. 77% efficiency 26,400 B.T.U.

When burning 4.4 pounds of wood per hour this model achieved top efficiency of 77%.

48000
46000

When burning 11 pounds of wood per hour this model achieved top B.T.U. output of 46,000

40% heat loss

40000

32000

26400

24000

16000

8000

0

B.T.U.

11 lbs./hr. 60% efficiency 46,000 B.T.U.

2.2 lb. 4.4 lb. 6.6 lb. 8.8 lb. 11.0

The Jøtul No. 606 achieved 77% efficiency. *Diagram courtesy of Kristia Associates, exclusive importers of Jøtul stoves, Portland, Maine 04104.*

The Jøtul No. 602 is only 18 inches long but will heat a medium-sized room. The ornamental bas-relief is by Ørnulf Bast. *Photo courtesy of Kristia Associates, exclusive importers of Jøtul stoves, Portland, Maine 04104.*

• How effective is your insulation? Are the storm windows tight and the door relatively draft-free?

• Are the winters in your area moderate and average-length or very cold and extended?

• Is your home located in a spot where it is windy a good part of the time? (That's another reason why fuel bills are high for one family and not nearly as high for their neighbors a half-mile away.)

With these questions answered, you determine that you need a stove capable of heating a room of 5,000 cubic feet. Now the choice of stoves has been narrowed down and significantly simplified, but there are still other matters to be sorted out.

Stove manufacturers' claims can be as extravagant

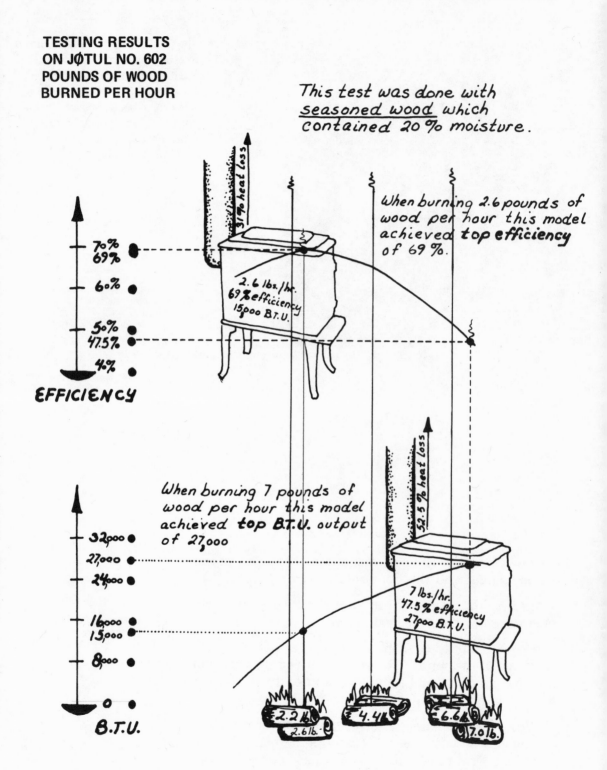

TESTING RESULTS ON JØTUL NO. 602 POUNDS OF WOOD BURNED PER HOUR

This test was done with seasoned wood which contained 20% moisture.

31% heat loss

When burning 2.6 pounds of wood per hour this model achieved **top efficiency** of 69%.

70%
69%

6%

5%
47.5%

4%

EFFICIENCY

2.6 lbs./hr.
69% efficiency
15,000 B.T.U.

When burning 7 pounds of wood per hour this model achieved **top B.T.U.** output of 27,000

52.5% heat loss

32,000
27,000
24,000

16,000
15,000

8,000

0

B.T.U.

7 lbs./hr.
47.5% efficiency
27,000 B.T.U.

2.2 lb.
2.6 lb.
4.4 lb.
6.6 lb.
7.0 lb.

The Jøtul No. 602 achieved 69% efficiency. *Diagram courtesy of Kristia Associates, exclusive importers of Jøtul stoves, Portland, Maine 04104.*

as the claims of any other manufacturer whether the product is an automobile or a ballpoint pen. A stove manufacturer may claim that *his* tree-burner is built as strong as a battleship, is the most efficient, most convenient, and the greatest value for the money—and he may be telling the truth. But you've heard it all before from the automobile and ballpoint pen people. At least this part of the stove-buying process is familiar to you, and you can move on to the considerations that really matter.

Recommending *the* best stove is obviously impossible. There are too many of them, they are too varied,

Height 31¾"
Weight 242 lbs.
Size 26½" x 12" inside

The *Nordic*, by Birmingham Stove & Range Co., is made of cast iron, with an upper chamber to radiate extra heat, and a baffle system. *Photo courtesy of Birmingham Stove & Range Co.*

and most will either not suit your purposes or will be too expensive. Consider which is the best stove for you. Do this by examining the basic types, how they work, and what features appeal to you.

The majority of woodburning stoves sold in the United States are airtights—also called controlled-burn stoves. They divide into two types: the domestic and the Scandinavian.

The second major category is the Franklin stove, which is manufactured by several domestic firms and a few foreign ones. Most of the Franklin stoves made today can be operated with the doors closed (which enables them to burn the wood very slowly, like an airtight) or with the doors open, burning the wood faster but reducing the amount of creosote accumulation in your flue (see Chapter 4). Having the stove doors open provides a fireplace effect for those who enjoy gazing into the flames—and who doesn't? It's relaxing, romantic, and at least as entertaining as watching the average television show.

You've probably heard the names of many stove types in addition to the Franklin and airtight: potbelly, barrel or drum, box, double chamber, parlor, and so on. These are named for their shape (potbelly), technical characteristic (double chamber), primary use (parlor location), or the material they are made from (the drum or barrel stove is made from an oil drum and a parts kit).

With only two major categories, the airtight and Franklin, we've narrowed the choices considerably. But there are many other types, sub-types, and one-of-a-kind stoves you may want to consider when you go shopping.

Like anything else, you get what you pay for when you buy a stove. Make certain you're not paying needless money for decorative trim or features unnecessary for your particular purpose. Several stoves are highly sophisticated in design and would be fine to own, but for your one-room, part-time use, buying them would merely be "overkill."

Once you've decided on a stove that will heat about 5,000 cubic feet of room space, you can zero in on size and price. Now you need to know the types, their characteristics, and the advantages and disadvantages of each.

The Morsø No. 1125, a combination stove of modern design, here operating as a Franklin stove. With the doors closed it functions as an airtight. *This material is published by permission of Lee Dora Gilchrist, Vice President, Southport Stoves, Inc.*

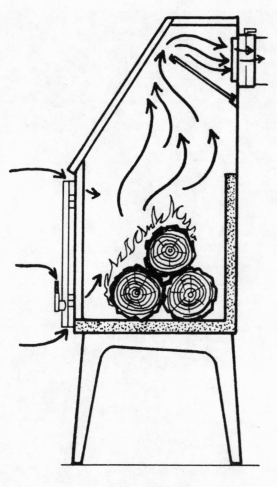

BACK-VENTED

The Morsø No. 1125, showing smoke-flow pattern. Wood can be placed horizontally or vertically, with the stove top- or back-vented. *This material is published by permission of Lee Dora Gilchrist, Vice President, Southport Stoves, Inc.*

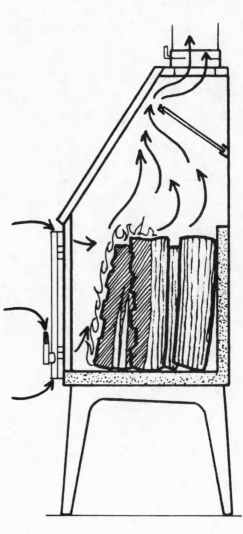

TOP-VENTED

The Scandinavian airtights—Jøtul, Morsø and Lange, among the best-known brands—are well made and efficient. They are constructed of cast iron, the most durable, warp-proof metal that can be used in a stove. Most Scandinavian airtights have a system of

The Jøtul No. 6 is called a "contemporary free-standing fireplace" by the manufacturer. It can be vented from the top directly into a chimney, or from behind with stovepipe. The doors open and close easily. *Photo courtesy of Kristia Associates, exclusive importers of Jøtul stoves, Portland, Maine 04104.*

The Jøtul No. 4 is an airtight when the unique sliding door is closed. *Photo courtesy of Kristia Associates, exclusive importers of Jøtul stoves, Portland, Maine 04104.*

baffles that forces heat to travel a long path, holding it in the stove for an extended period of time instead of allowing it to escape quickly through the chimney. A baffle system also forces volatiles to flow over the flames and burn as fuel, thus generating still more heat to be radiated from the stove to the room. The Scandinavian airtights also have manual draft controls to maintain adequate control over the fire.

Most of the Scandinavian brands are of the box stove type. Others are of a modern design. One attractive feature is that they are available not only in "basic black" but in several enamel colors at an extra cost that may fit well with your room decor.

With the door open, the Jøtul No. 4 becomes a Franklin stove. *Photo courtesy of Kristia Associates, exclusive importers of Jøtul stoves, Portland, Maine 04104.*

The principal disadvantage of the Scandinavian airtight is its price. One of these imports can cost upwards of one hundred dollars more than an American-made airtight or Franklin stove of comparable quality and efficiency. And although the Scandinavian stoves have characteristics that may appeal to you, these features must be weighed against the extra cost.

The main appeal of the American-made airtight is its lower cost. The reason for the price difference is that most of the domestic airtights are not made of cast iron but of steel plate or sheet steel. This is cheaper than cast iron construction because making and assembling a cast iron stove is time-consuming and mostly done by hand. The parts are molded in sand and then hand-machined for a precise fit.

The main criticism of sheet steel and steel plate is that the steel may warp and make your airtight stove no

The Thermomatic line of airtights is made in three sizes, to heat from two to ten rooms. *Photo courtesy of Thermomatic.*

An efficient radiant-heat wood-burner, Model R-77, by Shenandoah Manufacturing Co. *Photo courtesy of Shenandoah Manufacturing Co.*

longer so airtight. But this is unlikely to happen except under extremely hot temperatures. Many of the steel airtights are lined with firebrick insulation to help prevent warping. The more expensive stoves use a heavier-gauge steel which further reduces the possibility of warping. These stoves are about the same price as the Scandinavian stoves.

Cast iron also has its disadvantages. It is prone to damage by a sharp blow or by coming into contact with

The Knight Model No. 124 circulating heater is thermo-stat-controlled. *Photo courtesy of Birmingham Stove & Range Co.*

a cold object while hot. Building a fire in a very cold cast iron stove will crack the metal. You should not drop anything heavy on the stove, lean a frozen chunk of firewood against it, or light a fire after the stove has been standing in a cold room for any length of time. Certain tradeoffs must be considered.

Some of the better known and higher quality domestic steel airtights are made by Fisher, Hinckley, Mohawk Industries, New Hampshire Stove Works, and thermomatic. Several domestic manufacturers intend or have already begun to produce cast iron airtights. They are priced competitively and said to be as efficient and well made as the imported brands. By the time you are ready to buy your stove, you may have the best of both worlds.

The second major category of stoves combines the advantages of the airtight with a few appealing characteristics of its own. This is the well-known *Franklin*

The *Independence*, an airtight by The Stoveworks, shown with optional soapstone slabs which convert the stove to a circulating-type heater. *Photo courtesy of The Stoveworks.*

stove, also called the "stove-fireplace" or "combination stove." Among the companies manufacturing them are Vermont Castings, Inc., which makes the *Defiant* and its smaller version, the *Vigilant,* Birmingham Stove Works, Portland Stove Foundry, Inc., and Washington Stove Works. All provide a variety of sizes and models with unique features and accessories. Morso, Jotul, and Lange also make stove-fireplaces that operate in the same manner although their appearance is quite different from the traditional look of the American makes.

The Franklin-type stoves can be operated with the doors closed, which makes them function much like an airtight, or with the doors fully open.

The design of many of the contemporary Franklins has changed little in a couple of centuries, if at all. The *Eagle* Franklin stove, manufactured by the Portland Stove Foundry of Maine, uses patterns from plates designed in 1742. The *Olympic* Franklin stove is still made by the Washington Stove Works of Washington exactly as it was made by that company a century ago. They might be called "new antiques."

For many people, one of the main appeals of the Franklin stove is that when they leave the doors open, they are able to enjoy the sight of a crackling, open fire. When you've just come in from shoveling snow, building a snowman with the kids, or trudging a couple of miles in rain or slush from your disabled car, an open stove is a great place to warm up. During the holiday seasons and at parties, your open "fireplace" adds much to the festivities. Even if you plan only part-time use of your stove, these esthetic and emotional "extras" should be considered.

Another distinct type of woodburning stove is the *thermostat-controlled* or *circulating heater.* This is also called a *cabinet* stove. At first glance, it looks like a scaled-down version of the oil heater in your cellar. Since it works in a similar manner, many people prefer it to the more old-fashioned woodburning stove.

Besides having an automatic thermostat, this stove will burn unattended for many hours and is available with an optional air circulator to blow warm air into more than one room or warm the entire house (if it is one of the larger models).

Ashley, United States Stove, and Shenandoah are among the best-known manufacturers of the circu-

The Thermo-Control Model No. 100 is small, efficient, and lightweight.
Photo courtesy of Thermo-Control Wood Stoves.

The *Home Warmer* has a unique baffle and air-intake system; the upper chamber radiates additional heat. *Photo courtesy of New Hampshire Wood Stoves, Inc.*

The *Ponderosa*'s step design increases the heat-radiating area of the stove and provides a cooking surface. *Photo courtesy of Birmingham Stove & Range Co.*

Height 33½''
Weight 390 lbs.
Size 24¼'' x 13¾'' inside

lating stove. A number of companies don't even call them stoves but instead refer to them as heaters.

The main appeal of the circulating stove is convenience. It is automatic except for refueling; it is safe—sparks can't reach the floor; its exterior is not hot to the touch; and it burns clean without letting ashes into the room. A double chamber prevents this stove from getting hot on the outside. This is important if there are toddlers in the house. You will rarely, if ever, smell smoke from a thermostat-controlled stove. With its square, enameled cabinet, it is unobtrusive and blends in with any room's decor. If practicality and ease of operation are important, this type of stove should be considered. Its price is comparable to the airtight and the Franklin, and it heats just as efficiently.

Among the one-of-a-kind stoves are:

Better 'n Ben's which is actually a stove used in conjunction with a fireplace. An airtight metal plate seals the fireplace opening except for the exhaust vent. This stove-fireplace is similar to an airtight stove in function and appearance and combines a number of the advantages of both. If you have a fireplace, *Better 'n Ben's* is well worth considering.

The *Sevca* is an unusual stove because of its unconventional design, construction, and heating capacity. Made from recycled propane gas tanks because they are of thick, durable steel, the Sevca has a separate upper chamber that radiates heat from burning gases into the room. The Sevca is considered one of the most efficient of all types of stoves. It is also low priced.

Potbelly stoves are familiar to most Americans. They are the ones you see in the movies and on TV, in the old-time general stores with the town's good ol' boys sitting around swapping stories. The potbelly comes in various sizes and is produced by many stove companies. It is fine for a cabin in the woods or a drafty garage workshop where you need a good, hot fire for fairly brief periods of time, during a card game with your hunting buddies or while putting the snow tires on the car.

The *drum* or *barrel* stove is made from a recycled oil drum. The 55-gallon size is most common, although 30- and 15-gallon sizes are used. The drum stove is available assembled from a number of manufacturers, or you can buy a kit containing a cast iron door, legs,

Thermo-Control's Model No. 200 is a downdraft-type airtight available with optional hot water heat piping and hot water piping. *Photo courtesy of Thermo-Control Wood Stoves.*

The Shenandoah Model R-65 is an inexpensive wood and coal burner made especially for small homes, cabins, and garages. *Photo courtesy of Shenandoah Manufacturing Co.*

smoke collar, and stovepipe. Supply your own oil drum and the necessary cutting, drilling, and bolting, and you have a stove.

The *Reginald* is an airtight manufactured in Ireland rather than in Scandinavia. It is of high quality and comes in a kit form; you can save about fifty dollars over the factory-assembled version.

Many stove dealers have been in business for decades. They are experts at the installation, maintenance, and proper use of woodburners. Like other long-established businessmen, they are a part of their community and feel a responsibility toward their customers. They are willing to come to your home with advice on the type of stove you need. They will install it, help you get it functioning properly, and offer further advice. Of course they have the parts and staff when your stove needs repair.

The flip side of this situation is that since the woodburning stove boom of the past few years, dealers in other products have begun to sell stoves as a sideline. Obviously they are not likely to have the expertise possessed by people who have been in the stove business, perhaps exclusively, for many years.

You may have to do some traveling to find a stove dealer in your area. If so, take with you as much information as possible about your home: room size, type of insulation, and so on. The dealer will be willing to take the time to see that you buy the right stove.

If you have any friends or acquaintances who own woodburning stoves, get advice from them. Most stove-owners enjoy talking about them the way hobbyists enjoy talking about their hobbies. Write for brochures from the stove manufacturers listed in this book and in other books and magazines.

Chapter 3

Installing
Your Stove

You have joined the wood fuel renaissance and bought your stove, either from a local dealer or directly from a manufacturer. In a couple of weeks (if you've been smart and ordered in the spring or summer) the stove will arrive. Meanwhile, you've got some more homework to do—physical homework.

First you must find out where the stove will sit and radiate its bone-warming heat. Unfortunately you won't have any choice in this matter. The location of your chimney determines the location of your stove. (The chimney is that tall brick structure at the side of the house.) Your stove goes on whichever wall abuts the chimney. No, you can't simply cut a hole through a wall and poke the stovepipe through. There are quite a few city folks and suburbanites who think that's the way to do it. It is if you want to burn down your house. Besides smoke, very intense heat passes through the stovepipe, so a proper chimney connection must be made.

You must break through the wall, through the chimney, and, if your house is of recent vintage, through the flue, a lining inside the chimney, usually of

A parlor stove installation through a combustible wall, with proper clearances indicated. *Illustration by S. Mackay, courtesy of Northeast Regional Agricultural Engineering Service.*

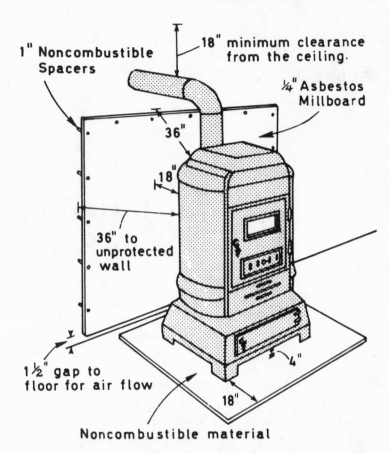

STOVE CLEARANCES

18" minimum clearance from the ceiling.

1" Noncombustible Spacers

¼" Asbestos Millboard

36"

18"

36" to unprotected wall

1½" gap to floor for air flow

4"

18"

Noncombustible material

ceramic material. Many old houses do not have chimney flues.

Since there is no way of knowing the exact structure of your walls—their age, whether they are plaster, laths, or wallboard—or the structure of the chimney and flue, it is impossible to make recommendations or give detailed instructions on how to do the job. Here is a general idea of what is involved in preparing to install a stove.

The wall must be broken through, making a hole not for the standard six- or eight-inch stovepipe but for a device called a *thimble* which is several inches larger in diameter than the stovepipe. The thimble is an airventilated and double-walled cylinder of metal or ceramic material. Inside it the stovepipe passes safely through the wall to the flue. This is the *chimney con-*

nector. The thimble acts as insulation, protecting combustible wall material from the stovepipe's heat.

Will your stovepipe be near a wooden beam? If so, you may need to pack additional insulation around this connector. Local laws may also require more protection.

Obviously this process is not simple. If it seems too much of a hassle, or you don't think you have the know-how to do a competent job, leave it all to the experts. A mason or his installation man (if you bought your stove from a local dealer) will be happy to do it. He will do the job right and, even more important, with safety uppermost in his mind. Anything touching or close to a hot stovepipe must be protected from the heat. Thus the thimble and whatever other insulating material is necessary.

If you live in an older house, the matter of flues and chimneys may be much simpler. Those big, old, rambling houses with many rooms were heated with wood stoves, possibly with one in every room, certainly one on every floor. Each room had a separate flue behind the wall. These flues formed a network that led to a large chimney. By now, of course, the old homestead has been converted to efficient central heating by you or a former owner, but those flues are still plugged up in the walls, their entrances hidden behind plaster, wallboard, and several layers of paint or wallpaper.

Depending on how careful the plasterer was, you may be able to see traces of these flue holes. If so, your stove installation will be much easier. All you have to do is find the flue holes, chip away the plaster or whatever is hiding it, and you've got your chimney connector. If the plaster is very thick, or wallboard or wood paneling has been installed over the flues, it won't be that easy. Start tapping with a rubber mallet or something that will enable you to hear a difference in sounds when you tap. Flue holes are usually thirty inches or more above the floor. Good luck.

If your home has fireplaces, you've got it made. Even if they've been bricked up, it's not hard to open a fireplace. Your stove can then be vented through the fireplace flue with very little work.

Before making any installation, it is mandatory that you inspect your chimney and flue. For the efficient and safe operation of any stove, the flue or chimney must be reasonably clean of creosote and carbon deposits. If your fireplace and flue haven't been used in decades, they may have to be cleaned.

Inspecting your chimney is reasonably simple: you can look straight up inside the fireplace. If you see lots of daylight and blue sky, the chimney is clean enough. If your chimney has a clean-out door outside (toward the bottom), open it and check by holding a hand mirror inside. Do you see daylight and blue sky? Your chimney is clean.

If your flue has a bend in it, or there is no clean-out door, you've got to climb onto the roof with a long rope and a good-sized flashlight or, even better, a bulb on a long wire (the type auto mechanics use). Lower the flashlight or bulb down the flue, and check along the sides for build-up.

If this sounds like too much work, call a mason to inspect the chimney for creosote and other deposits. He will also check your chimney's structure for weak spots and cracks.

If you have a fairly new house that has never had anything but oil or gas central heating, your flue won't need any work. These fuels are relatively clean burning and leave no creosote. (Chimney-cleaning, something you can do with a minimum of effort, is detailed in Chapter 7.) If you find more gunk up there than you want to clean out yourself, hire a chimney sweep. Yes, there has been a chimney sweep renaissance too, and there may be one in your town. Your stove dealer should know someone qualified to do the work.

Another problem you may face is whether or not your flue can handle both your central heating system and one or more wood stoves. The subject is controversial. One group of experts says it's something that should never be done. Another group says it is all right if your flue is large enough; you don't run both the furnace and the wood stove at full capacity for a long time; and the two heater vents are not too close together in the flue. To show just how controversial the matter is, the National Fire Prevention Association includes in its standards the recommendation that this never be done—then gives instructions on how to do it. Again, rely on the local stove dealer if there is one in your area. Your volunteer fire department may also be able to give you advice. If you live in a good-sized town or

city, there may be a printed fire department code, and
you may discover that there are restrictions on the use
of woodburning stoves. It is possible that venting two
heating appliances of any kind into one flue is illegal.
In that case you would have to build a new chimney or
install a second flue inside your old chimney. This can
be a major expense even if you do the work yourself

A circulating heater installed on a
brick/cement base, vented through
a brick chimney flue. *Photo courtesy of Birmingham Stove & Range
Co.*

The Better 'n' Ben's fireplace stove is a domestic airtight designed specifically for use with an existing fireplace. *Diagram courtesy of C & D Distributors, Inc.*

without hiring a contractor. The materials aren't cheap. All of this depends on the extent of your plans to use wood heat.

Chances are that if your flue is large enough and in good condition, and if you don't figure on operating both your furnace and wood stove at peak capacity for hours at a time, your flue can handle them both.

If you plan to install a woodburning stove in a vacation cabin in the woods or in your garage-workshop area, your chimney problem is less complex. You can probably do the work yourself or with a friend or two. All the rules of stove installation apply, of course, even if you're putting in only a small potbelly or drum stove.

You may be able to use only stovepipe as a flue, enough to extend from the stove—which should be well away from any wooden wall or beams—to at least two feet from an outer wall of the structure, and then up until it is a few feet higher than the roof. You will need that thimble and an insulated shield for the inner wall.

Keep in mind that stovepipe is not rugged enough for an outside flue that will be used constantly. Wind, rain, snow, and ice take their toll. An outside flue constructed of stovepipe must be dismantled, checked, and cleaned after each extended use or after several brief uses (over a few weekends or several evenings). This is for safety and to prevent the flue's rapid deterioration. *Wood Heat* by John Vivian (see Bibliography) contains a section with excellent do-it-yourself instructions, clear diagrams, and a list of materials for building simple, light-use flues.

Once the chimney and flue problems are solved, you must heat-proof the wall behind the stove and the floor around it.

Most stove manufacturers recommend in their instruction manuals that you locate your stove at least thirty-six inches from the wall. If it must be placed closer, add a protective shield of insulating material on the wall behind it. With such protection, the stove is safe a foot or so away from the wall.

There are various types of insulating shield made especially for this purpose: metal, asbestos, or a combination of the two. They should be installed with spacers that allow for a few inches of air behind the shield. Without air space, the shield itself will conduct heat to the wall.

As for floor protection, many stoves have legs that keep the stove bed, and thus the heat, several inches above the floor. The possibility of the floor overheating, being damaged, or catching fire is remote. However, as a precaution it makes sense to place the stove on some protective material such as galvanized sheet metal. Select a piece of suitably heavy gauge and a size large enough to extend a foot or so beyond the back and sides of the stove, and eighteen inches or more in front if you have a stove with a front-opening door. This protects the floor from sparks and ashes.

A more ambitious and better-looking floor shield can be made from bricks, flagstone, slate, concrete, or any stone or masonry material. With ingenuity you can add to the decor of your living room.

There it is—your wood burner, sitting rock-steady on its protective floor base, the stovepipe passing safely through the wall and the asbestos wall shield into your clean flue. You've got kindling, some medium-sized split-wood, several logs of the right size, and newspaper. Oh yes, matches. You're ready for your first fire.

• Follow the stove's instruction manual. If the stove is made of cast iron, it will need careful breaking in. Cast iron must be "seasoned" until it gets used to the expansions and contractions it undergoes with heat fluctuations. Therefore the first dozen fires in a cast iron stove—or any metal stove—must be fairly small. One thing you must never do with any stove is build a roaring fire when the stove is completely cold from sitting in a cold room.

• After following the owner's manual as to adjusting dampers and thermostat (if your stove has one), lay some crumpled newspaper (avoid coated magazine paper) on the floor of the firebox, and several sticks of kindling on top of the paper.

• If you have a tall stove, stack some thicker kindling on top of the thin kindling to make an Indian teepee. In square or rectangular stoves, lay the wood flat, crisscrossing it to leave air spaces between the sticks.

• Finished? Then light up.

• Once the kindling is burning well (you may have to readjust the dampers) lay on a few sticks of thicker wood.

Soon you'll have a moderate fire just right for breaking in the stove and keeping you warm too.

Again it must be stressed that the break-in period for a stove is important. No one in his right mind drives a new car from the showroom straight to the interstate highway to "open her up and see what she'll do." The same caution should be used with a stove. You'll have it for a long time—far longer than you'll have the average car—so take your time and break it in properly.

You might run into a little trouble with the first fires. For example:

• The owner's manual says your stove will hold a fire for several hours, but your fires are going out in maybe half that time. Experiment with the damper openings and readjust the thermostat.

• Your wood is burning too fast. Again, experiment with your stove's dampers. Are you using softwood

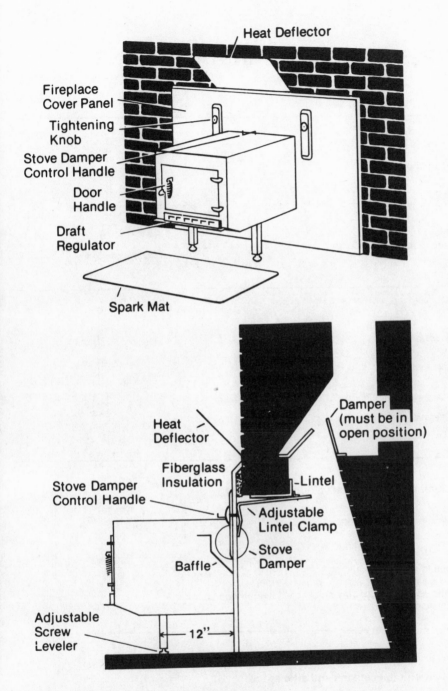

Heat Deflector

Fireplace
Cover Panel

Tightening
Knob

Stove Damper
Control Handle

Door
Handle

Draft
Regulator

Spark Mat

Heat
Deflector

Damper
(must be in
open position)

Fiberglass
Insulation

Stove Damper
Control Handle

Lintel

Adjustable
Lintel Clamp

Stove
Damper

Baffle

Adjustable
Screw
Leveler

12"

Installation is simple, with combined Better 'n' Ben's stove and cover
panel fastened in front of the chimney opening without masonry altera-
tions. *Diagram courtesy of C & D Distributors, Inc.*

TYPES OF CHIMNEY INSTALLATIONS

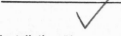

Installation #1
Flat ceiling with attic space.
Parts needed:
1 - Flush support box
1 - Roof Flashing
1 - Storm Collar
1 - Rain Cap
Enough insulated pipe to reach total height.

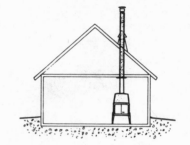

Installation #2
Open beam or cathedral ceiling.
Parts needed:
1 - Long Support Box
1 - Roof Flashing
1 - Storm Collar
1 - Rain Cap
Enough insulated pipe to reach total height.

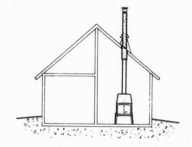

Installation #3
Porch or room addition with open beam ceiling and flat roof.
Parts needed:
1 - Long Support Box
1 - Storm Collar
1 - Roof Flashing
1 - Rain Cap
Enough insulated pipe to reach total height.
NOTE: If installation is within 10' of vertical walls, dormers
    or higher roofs, increase chimney height to 2' higher than
    any point 10' away.

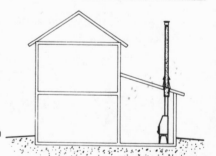

Installation #4
Multi-floor installation with flat ceilings and attic space.
Parts needed:
1 - Flush Support Box
1 - Fire Stop (for each *additional* ceiling)
1 - Roof Flashing
1 - Storm Collar
1 - Rain Cap
Enough insulated pipe to reach total height.

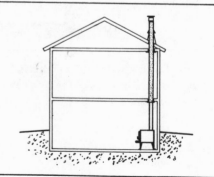

Installation #5
Through the wall — up the outside of the house — through a roof overhang.
Parts needed:
2 - Wall Spacers or Collar Spacers
1 - Insulated Tee
1 - Wall Band or Strap Spacer for each 8' of wall
1 - Firestop
1 - Roof Flashing
1 - Storm Collar
1 - Rain Cap
Enough insulated pipe to reach total height.

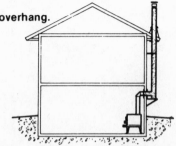

Installation #6
Through the wall — up the outside of the house — no roof overhang
Parts needed:
2 - Wall Spacers or Collar Spacers
1 - Insulated Tee
1 - Tee Support
1 - Wall Band or Strap Spacer for each 8' of wall
1 - Rain Cap
Enough insulated pipe to reach total height.

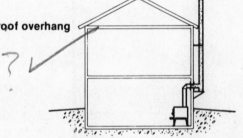

Installation #7
Through a combustible wall into a masonry chimney.
Parts needed:
2 - Wall Spacers or Collar Spacers.

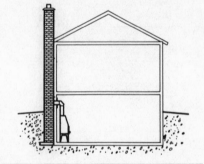

Installation #8
Offset installation — bypassing the ridge (or obstacle in the attic).
Parts needed:
1 - Flush Support Box
2 - Insulated Elbows
1 - 12'' pcs. Insulated Pipe
1 - Roof Flashing
1 - Storm Collar
1 - Rain Cap
Enough insulated pipe to complete the total run.

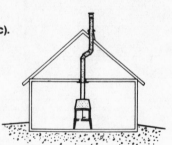

Installation is possible in any type of house, with either the existing chimney or the use of a newly installed prefabricated chimney. *This material is published by permission of Lee Dora Gilchrist, Vice President, Southport Stoves, Inc.*

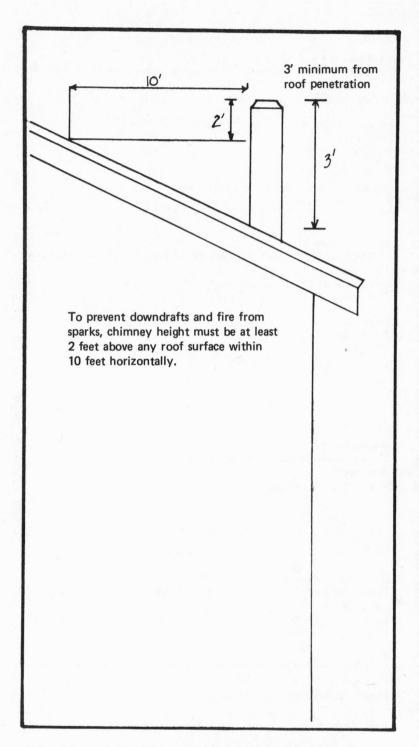

To prevent downdrafts and fire from sparks, chimney height must be at least 2 feet above any roof surface within 10 feet horizontally.

These chimney height figures are recommended by the National Fire Protection Association. *Illustration by S. Mackay, courtesy of Northeast Regional Agricultural Engineering Service.*

rather than hardwood? Softwood burns fast. That may be why your fires are going out, too. See Chapter 6 before you buy any more wood.

• Your stove smokes. If the stovepipe was installed properly, the flue is clean, and you are using the stove dampers correctly, the smoke may result from your stove's needing more oxygen. Open a window in the room. Well-insulated homes can be remarkably air-tight. If your stove seems to smoke only on windy days, the wind is "pushing" smoke back down the chimney. All you need is a chimney cap, a minor expense.

No serious problems will arise if your stove has been properly installed, and you are following the owner's manual. Of course, as with any newly-purchased item—especially one you are unfamiliar with—unforeseen difficulties may arise. If something about your stove's operation has you stumped, call your dealer or the manufacturer for advice.

Chapter 4

Stove Safety

In the installation and use of a woodburning stove—actually any stove in any kind of structure—safety cannot be overstressed. When using a stove for any purpose, you are literally playing with fire. At the risk of giving the prospective stove-buyer second thoughts, the negative aspects (to put it delicately) must be dealt with.

The sudden upsurge in the use of wood stoves has led to an increase in the number of house fires. Public safety officials in New England, for example, have stated that, in many cases, these fires are due to improper installation and use of woodburning stoves. They also place part of the blame on lax building inspection. Safety inspectors are apparently failing to require homeowners to obey local laws involving wood stoves. Because of the sharp increase in wood stove use, inspections may have fallen far behind.

As in the case of any business which begins to boom, a few fly-by-night operators rush in, turn out shoddy or ill-conceived products, sell them to the unknowledgeable, and then disappear with the profits. The wood stove business is no exception. A small minority of manufacturers is probably cutting corners by turning out faulty stoves or stoves that lack essential safety features that are often required by state or local laws.

If the wood stove boom continues—and there is good reason to believe it will—new regulations and stricter enforcement of existing ones will no doubt be in effect by the time you read this. That is all to the good. You and your family will be safer, but there is much that you yourself can do to assure that safety. Improper or careless installation or use of a wood stove can burn down your house. It is that simple.

Most of us under the age of fifty have always lived in an age of technology. A certain amount of safety has been built into the mechanical and electronic devices we use every day. We take this for granted and don't give it a thought. In homes with central heating, electric or oil furnaces have fail-safe devices that protect our lives and property, but with a wood stove, the user is the most dependable safety device. The human mind, functioning properly, protects us best. A car accident is, more often than not, the fault of the driver, not of the vehicle. It is usually human error, neglect, or carelessness in the use of a wood stove that is responsible for a fire, but it does not have to be that way.

Before the advent of central heating, the number of house fires was small in proportion to the number of wood stoves and fireplaces in use. This was because people had an ingrained knowledge of how to treat their wood stoves: with forethought, respect, and a healthy amount of fear. The safety precautions to be taken now are about the same as those taken a century or more ago. They are simple enough.

If you are handy with tools and decide to install the stove yourself, follow the manufacturer's instructions to the letter. The manufacturer is the expert. He knows his stove best and is reputable and responsible.

Don't take any shortcuts. That could be costly. If your dealer installs the stove, don't allow *him* to take any shortcuts. Check the work against the stove owner's manual to see that it has been done properly. A conscientious dealer will make sure your stove is correctly installed, but no one is perfect. If the dealer makes an error or is momentarily careless, it's *your* house that will be lost.

Before you touch a match to your paper and kind-

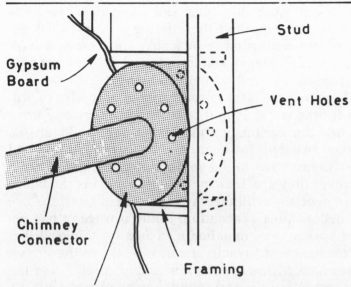

A ventilated thimble permits the stove pipe to pass safely through a combustible wall.

- Stud
- Gypsum Board
- Vent Holes
- Chimney Connector
- Framing

Thimble diameter should be three times the diameter of the stove pipe.

A vital factor in stove safety is the use of a thimble to protect combustible wall material. *Illustration by S. Mackay, courtesy of Northeast Regional Agricultural Engineering Service.*

ling, have at least one fire extinguisher in the house. Make certain that everyone in your family knows how to use it. Most extinguishers made for household use are simple enough for a fairly young child to use.

Keep the extinguisher in an easily accessible place where anyone can get to it without passing the stove. A good spot is on a wall between the room where the stove is located and an exit from the house. If possible, keep it near your telephone, so you can call the fire department and operate the extinguisher at the same time. Sound impossible? Give it a run-through. In a house fire, minutes mean a lot.

A second fire extinguisher is a good idea. This spare might be located in or near your bedroom or the staircase if you keep your wood stove burning all night (as many people do if it is their main source of heat).

A smoke detector is worthwhile too although it will be necessary to place it outside the room where the stove is located so it doesn't pick up the normal amount of smoke coming from the stove.

Together with the fire extinguisher and smoke detector, a plain, old-fashioned bucket of sand or water can be kept near the stove. Don't forget to refill the water bucket now and then. Being a mechanical device, a fire extinguisher or smoke detector can malfunction. Well-placed water and sand will at least control a small fire and minimize damage.

Though unpleasant to contemplate, it is wise to prepare for the worst even if you don't have a wood stove and are not seriously considering one. Hold an occasional fire drill for every member of the family and show them how to leave the house quickly from wherever they are. Designate a place outside the house where everyone will meet in the event of a serious fire that necessitates evacuation. Many a tragedy has occurred when one member of a family, thinking that another member, usually a child, is still in the house, rushes back inside to save him and is killed. Then the child appears, safe and sound, having already left the house.

There are other precautions to be taken, most of them involving common sense.

• Never use lighter fluid, gasoline, or other combustibles to start a fire in your stove or "help it along."

• Don't store any kind of flammable liquid in the same room with a wood stove.

• If you have a Franklin stove, close the doors or place the fire screen over the front of the stove when you leave the room for any length of time. Sparks can jump a fair distance; they can even pass through a fire screen. Go with the possibility principle.

• Don't place things like wet socks, mittens, or shoes to dry on or above the stove. A number of stoves are equipped with a rack that swings out for drying small items of clothing. Use it. Otherwise you may end up not with dried clothes but with charred clothes—and a charred house.

• Check your stovepipe and chimney connector regularly for wear, corrosion, or any abnormality such as chinks in the masonry or sealant around the thimble or a loose stovepipe.

• When you empty the ashes, place them in a metal container. Live coals may be buried among them.

• If your stove can be used for cooking, fine, but be careful of grease—it is flammable. If you have a Franklin-type stove, it might seem like a good idea to toast marshmallows or barbecue hot dogs. The kids will think it's great fun, but barbecues are safer outside in the barbecue pit.

Even the youngest child knows what "hot" is, but he may not recognize less familiar dangers inherent in a wood stove. It isn't likely to occur to him that his warm, secure home can catch fire. It is up to you to see that he has some understanding of the potential danger of that exciting toy that makes the living room so toasty warm and pleasant. This is done best by example. If you are cautious, he will be cautious. If he sees you disobeying your own safety rules, he will disobey them, too.

If you have a toddler in the house, rig up some sort of protective barrier around the stove. It can be something collapsible that can be stored when the little one is in bed for the night. A child younger than about three

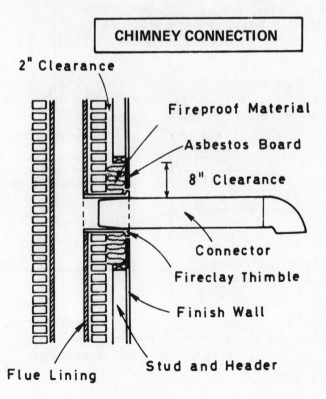

Fig. 4-2

Fireproof material and air space are essential wherever heat is radiated near a wall or ceiling. *Illustration by S. Mackay, courtesy of Northeast Regional Agricultural Engineering Service.*

years isn't all that stable when he walks, runs, and plays. He can easily fall against the stove and be burned.

Never let young children put anything like trash or pieces of paper into the stove. They are bound to enjoy this and may do it when their parents are out of the room. Besides the risk of the child's being burned, some valuable possession of yours may go up in smoke.

It is a good idea to have a young child help when the time comes to place another log on the fire. Make this a special sort of ritual, something he understands is

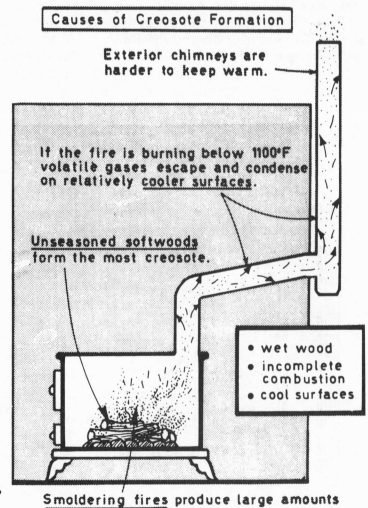

Causes of Creosote Formation

Exterior chimneys are harder to keep warm.

If the fire is burning below 1100°F volatile gases escape and condense on relatively cooler surfaces.

Unseasoned softwoods form the most creosote.

- wet wood
- incomplete combustion
- cool surfaces

Smoldering fires produce large amounts of creosote.

Fig. 4-3

With proper installation, precautions, and well-seasoned wood, most creosote formation can be avoided. *Illustration by S. Mackay, courtesy of Northeast Regional Agricultural Engineering Service.*

always done with a parent and never alone. This way you'll give him the feeling that he is contributing and also allay his curiosity about the stove and how it works.

Those are the safety measures involved in everyday use of a stove. There are also long-term precautions that are, in part at least, maintenance measures directly involved with safety.

One of the greatest dangers with a wood stove over a period of time is a chimney fire which is literally a fire in the chimney that can spread to the rest of your house or shower sparks onto your neighbors' houses and the surrounding backyards, woods, or fields. Actually it is not the chimney that is on fire. Chimneys and flues are made of masonry, steel, or a ceramic material, none of which burn. What catches fire is a tar-like substance called creosote, a by-product of burning wood. A certain amount of creosote build-up in a chimney or flue is unavoidable.

Hardwoods produce the least amount of creosote; the softest woods produce the most. There are many gradations in between. Damp wood produces more creosote than properly seasoned (dried) wood. Airtight and circulating stoves are the most efficient and convenient of woodburners, but the way they function is very conducive to creosote formation.

Creosote forms most readily when wood is burned slowly for a long time, there is little oxygen in the stove, and the chimney has been allowed to cool off. This is exactly what happens in an airtight stove that burns overnight. It has been heavily fueled, the draft is turned down so there is minimal air flow, the fire is merely smoldering, and the chimney cools off.

Incompletely burned vapors from the wood enter the cool flue, condense, and adhere to its sides in the form of a dark brown, gooey material. When the flue warms up later, the creosote dries into flakes which continue to stick to the flue. It is then flammable and becomes dangerous when enough builds up. Then one day, when it is unusually cold and there's a really hot fire in your stove, the creosote catches and burns like any other fuel.

The great danger is that if your chimney is old, has no flue, or has defects you are not aware of (cracks, holes or weakness in the masonry), the flames can pass through the chimney to beams in the roof or walls. Chimney fires are fortunately rare and usually burn themselves out, provided there is only a small amount of creosote built up in the chimney.

It is essential that your chimney and flue are kept in good condition. If you have an airtight or circulating stove, don't use it in closed-down condition all of the time. Allow some air to get in now and then to slow the creosote build-up. This will decrease the stove's efficiency somewhat, but that is a small price to pay for safety.

There are products available whose manufacturers claim they prevent the buildup of creosote. While many stove users swear by them, about as many others won't use them. You might try one of the products. Your best bet with any stove is to keep your flue, chimney, and stovepipes clean. If you can't find a mason or professional chimney sweep, consider doing the job yourself. It isn't as difficult as it seems. Chapter 5 gives the details.

Besides yourself and your neighbors, your insurance company is interested in safety. Check your home insurance policy. You will probably find a clause requiring you to notify the company if you plan to make any changes in your home that might affect safety. This doesn't necessarily mean your premium will be raised, but if you fail to comply and there is a fire, they may not pay for the damages. They certainly will not pay if your woodburning stove was installed in violation of state or local safety regulations.

Chapter 5

Wood Is Wood, Right? Wrong

When was the last time you did any deep thinking about trees? Quite a while, probably. We all see them, of course. If you live in a rural or suburban area, they are difficult to miss. If you're a city-dweller and occasionally get to the country, you take special notice of trees because they are such a rarity in the city, where you see them only in parks or in rows along the sidewalk, surrounded by little fences to protect them from dogs. Few of us give any thought to trees themselves, but now that you are or soon will be the owner of a woodburning stove, some thought about trees—specifically trees as fuel—is in order.

Paper is made from wood. Wood is used to build our homes and our furniture. Our railroads run on steel rails laid over wooden ties. We get countless chemicals from wood: turpentine, acetone, methyl alcohol, acetic acid. All are vital to industry. Useful stuff, wood. It is strong, buoyant, flexible, durable, and almost impervious to the elements and most insects; it lasts indefinitely.

Wood can be bent, carved, and molded into almost any conceivable shape. From wood we make everything from buildings to boats to toothpicks. We burn it to keep warm.

Among Americans concerned with the environment, the question arises as to whether or not it is ecologically wise to promote the large-scale use of wood as fuel. True, trees are what is called a "renewable resource"—they grow back. Still, what happens if woodburning stove technology advances so quickly that wood stoves become as efficient, convenient, and safe to use as other types of heaters? What if tens of millions of American homeowners (as well as industrial plants) switch to woodburning stoves and furnaces? Suppose we begin to burn wood as wastefully as we consume heating oil? Many of us are still careless about insulation and overheat our homes even now, during a continuing energy crisis.

For years the fuel companies, whether the giant oil- and gas-producers or the electric utilities, have encouraged fuel waste by convincing us there was a supply of cheap fuel that would last until the end of the world. Few of us gave a thought to the idea that one day gasoline would be edging up toward a dollar a gallon, and that our home heating bills—oil or gas or electric—would double within a couple of winters. In the colder areas of the nation, it became a case of pay up or freeze to death in the dark. A shortage of fuel? Incredibly high prices? No way, we said. Then along came that "ol' devil" energy crisis.

If there is a sudden change in woodburning stove technology—"sudden" meaning within five to ten years, as such changes generally go—will the forests be depleted? With increased demand, will the price of wood fuel go as high, or higher, than the price of our other fuels? Will we see "tree rustlers" slipping into our forests or our modest two-acre woodlots to steal trees?

None of this is likely to happen. First, it is unimaginable that tens of millions of Americans are going to scrap their oil, gas, or electric central heating systems and go all-out for wood heat. Even now it is possible to convert heaters to woodburners or buy wood furnaces or even combination oil/wood furnaces and thumb our noses at the oil companies, but not many people are doing so.

Second, if wood were seriously to begin competing

with oil as fuel for any reason, Exxon, Mobil, Amoco, and the other oil companies would soon own every forest, woodlot, tree, bush, scrap of driftwood, and every splinter down to our discarded toothpicks. For all we know, these giant corporations are already buying up choice tracts of forest just in case. Would Exxon, for example, fail to hedge its bets? Not likely. They would certainly protect their investment by carefully man-

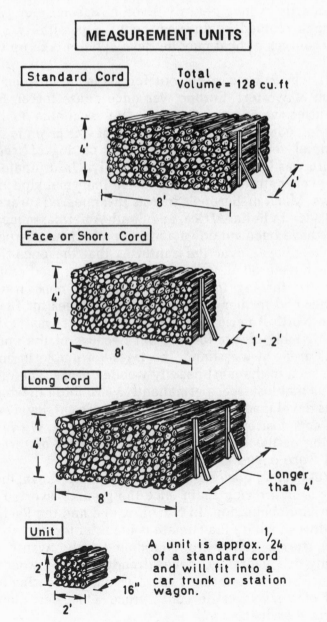

MEASUREMENT UNITS

Standard Cord — Total Volume = 128 cu. ft

4' / 8' / 4'

Face or Short Cord

4' / 8' / 1'- 2'

Long Cord

4' / 8' / Longer than 4'

Unit

2' / 2' / 16"

A unit is approx. 1/24 of a standard cord and will fit into a car trunk or station wagon.

A number of states require by law that wood be sold only by the cord or fraction of a cord. In practice, however, other standards may be used. *Illustration by S. Mackay, courtesy of Northeast Regional Agricultural Engineering Service.*

aging their holdings. Prices might rise, and we would be forced to change our wasteful habits.

A more likely assessment is that within ten years or so, our domestic petroleum supplies will begin to run so short that we will have to import that high-priced fuel: oil. Homeowners will feel the pinch again and begin another wood stove renaissance. Will our forests suffer?

Even with a serious future energy crisis, it isn't likely that many Americans will turn to wood fuel, either voluntarily or involuntarily. Even now, solar energy is being developed, geothermal heat is a possibility, and new sources of heat may be developed to take up the slack.

However, concern for our forests is not misplaced. Much of western Europe was once dense forest. For centuries, wood was the only fuel available to the growing population there. No thought was given to the eventual result of the unrestricted cutting of trees; nature was left to replenish the supply. Unfortunately, not even nature can create faster than mankind destroys. Much of Europe's forests disappeared forever.

Today in India, Africa, and South America, so many trees have been cut down and not replenished by people in villages over the centuries that the once-rich lands have eroded, will no longer support food crops, and are turning into desert. Villagers must travel farther and farther from home to find trees for fuel.

In North America we were well on our way to depleting most of our forests, but because of the enormous areas of forestland, the trees were able to hold their own in the most heavily-wooded areas. The only places that lost trees permanently were those in which cities developed or where the trees were cut down and the roots destroyed so that crops could grow. With the coming of the automobile, countless acres of forestland were paved to make highways.

Yet even in places where trees were cut down, they were soon growing again once the ground reverted to its original condition. In New England and the Pacific Northwest, where the climate is ideal for the growth of trees, farms that were abandoned only twenty or twenty-five years ago have already become wooded again. Farmers had spent years gradually clearing the land of trees so cattle could graze. Once left alone, nature took its course.

The environmentalists can rest easy. Most commercial interests that own forests have seen the light and have ceased or modified such destructive practices as clear-cutting forests. They belatedly realized they were destroying their very source of profit.

Stoves are so efficient today that even if millions of Americans converted to wood fuel, they would still be burning less wood than was burned a century ago when stoves and fireplaces were inefficient and homes were poorly insulated.

Wood comes close to being the "infinite fuel." With proper care of our existing tree supply—reforestation, a cessation of wasteful lumbering practices, recycling of paper—it can become an important supplement to other fuels.

The infinite fuel is, in effect, stored energy from the sun, the source of almost all our energy, whether it comes from wood, oil, coal, gas, or electricity. Only nuclear power does not originate from the sun. While oil and coal are gone forever once they are used, trees can be replanted to begin the cycle again.

The chemical components of the various woods are basically similar, but for our consideration of wood as fuel we can divide it into two general types: hardwoods and softwoods. There are many gradations between the extremes.

In the northern and midwestern portions of America, hardwoods predominate. As we go farther south and west, softwoods increase. If you live in a section of the country where plenty of hardwood grows, you have the best kind of wood fuel. Your only concern is obtaining the wood as cheaply and easily as possible.

There are two ways to get wood for your stove. The easy way is to buy it by the cord and have it delivered. Have the cord cut into four-foot lengths, which will then have to be sawed to the proper length for your stovebed, into foot-long logs. Either way, you should be getting a cord of wood. A cord is an exact measurement: a stack of logs, reasonably solidly piled, four feet high by eight feet long by four feet deep. These figures may vary, but they should come to 128 cubic feet. The weight of a cord of wood (an average, since types of wood vary in weight) is about *two tons*. If you've been thinking of taking your sturdy little hatchback to the woodman and loading it with a cord of wood to save the delivery charge, forget it. The wood will weigh more than the car. The delivery charge isn't much anyway, usually around ten dollars.

The price of a cord of wood varies. With the wood stove renaissance in full swing, the price of wood has gone up with the increased demand. A cord may cost anywhere from fifty to two hundred dollars, depending on the type of wood, the area where you live, and the rate of inflation. The price is also affected by whether the wood has been cut into neat four-foot or one-foot lengths or is sold "rough," in irregularly shaped logs of various lengths which you'll have to cut to proper size yourself. You'll save money if you buy in the spring or early summer. Wait until fall or winter, and you'll pay more. Another consideration is that if you buy your wood off-season, it will have a few months to dry and will be ready for burning when you need it.

As in buying anything, shop around. If you're fortunate enough to live in an area where there are several wood dealers, you can do a little wheeling and dealing. Be sure to ask these questions:

What kind of wood is being sold? The softwoods should be cheaper than the hardwoods, and you are well advised to know the difference between them (see the chart at the end of this chapter). You'll need softer wood for starting a fire and harder wood for long burning. This can be important if you don't plan to use your stove full time and will frequently be starting new fires.

Does the price include delivery?

More importantly, does the price include stacking the logs? The dealer may simply drive up and unload the logs as close to your house as he can get. Then it will be up to you to play lug-a-log, carrying those heavy logs to where you want them. You can avoid a couple of afternoons of hard labor by coming to an agreement with the wood dealer about stacking.

As mentioned earlier, different parts of the country grow different types of trees. You can't walk into a wood dealer's and order a cord or two of ash or hickory logs if they don't grow in your area. You may have to settle for wood that isn't among the best for fuel.

There are special precautions for city-dwellers to

take when buying wood. Woodburning stoves are not common in large cities, but a number of people who own brownstones or live in large renovated lofts (in which the supply of heat isn't always the best) are now turning to stoves to supplement their regular heating source. Many older buildings, especially in Manhattan's Greenwich Village and Chelsea areas, have working fireplaces. The tenants in these buildings are often faced with old furnaces that constantly break down. The furnace sits until the repairman returns from his vacation in Acapulco to order a part that is handcrafted only in a one-man machine shop in the Canadian Yukon. Meanwhile the tenants freeze—unless they have fuel for their fireplaces.

To the unknowing city-dweller, a cord of wood may be nothing more than six logs a foot long and six inches in circumference, tied together and sold at the corner grocery for five dollars. That's like burning money.

If you have a wood stove or a fireplace or two, it's worth driving fifteen or twenty miles into the suburbs or the country to find your wood. Load your car with enough logs to last for a couple of winters. You'll find better wood at much lower prices than you will in the city. Just make certain it will fit into the fireplace or stove bed. The neighbors may object to your chopping wood in your apartment.

The cheapest way to obtain wood unfortunately involves the most physical labor. You must go to where the wood is literally lying around waiting for someone to haul it away—free, or at nominal charge.

You may have friends or relatives who own more than just an acre or two of land, and this land may have many trees. We're not suggesting that you ask if you may chop down their trees. But in a wooded area there is always a certain amount of dead wood on the ground; trees have died for one reason or another or been blown down by windstorms. Rather than pay to have this dead wood hauled away, the landowner has left it to rot. Such wood often impedes the growth of other trees and vegetation. Tell your friend or relative of that fact and generously offer to haul the wood away. It may not be the best wood for fuel, especially if it is rotting, but it is free except for the gasoline you'll use to drive it home. You may be lucky enough to find wood that is already seasoned but not rotten. Even landowners you don't know will permit you to clean up their woods—if they don't own wood stoves themselves.

Telephone and utility companies periodically trim branches and even cut down trees that interfere with their wires. Call your local company and ask what areas are due for trimming and cutting so you can be the first wood stove owner to get there. They'll be only to happy to avoid the cost of hauling the logs away themselves. If new power lines are being installed in your neck of the woods, you can have a field day. Utilities cut a swath through the woods, felling trees not only where the poles will be installed but for several yards on either side of the route. With a few trips and a lot of work, you may get enough wood to last you a few winters.

Any time after a heavy, windy rainstorm, you'll find that entire trees have been blown down. Local authorities usually arrange to get the trees out of the way, dragging them off to the side of the road so they don't impede traffic. Go get 'em. Of course the wood will be wet, but it will dry out—and it is free.

Even if you're a little late getting to the storm area, don't be disappointed. Drive to the local dump or landfill. You're likely to find the tree branches there—unless the wood stove renaissance has caught on in your town. But if not you'll find your fuel. To the town administrators it's a nuisance, but to you it's money in the bank. As a bonus you'll find that the wood has been cut to manageable sizes.

If you live in a rural area, another good source of wood is the state and national parks and forests. They also have trees that are blown down by storms or killed by disease or insects. These trees have to be removed so they don't harm other vegetation or present a hazard to campers, hikers, and other visitors. Since the increase in wood stove use, park authorities have been permitting people to remove the trees in specially designated areas of the parks and forests. But before you load your axe and chainsaw into the station wagon and head for your nearest park, telephone and find out the policy in that particular park and whether there is enough wood to make the trip worthwhile.

Lumberyards, sawmills, and furniture manufacturing plants are also good sources, but the wood may not be the best kind for fuel. They'll be only too happy to let you haul away their scrap wood, but don't bother with the softwoods, except what you can use for kindling.

If there is an orchard near you, contact the owner. Most fruit trees must be pruned periodically. Older, less productive trees are also cut down and replaced. Find out when he'll be doing this work, and maybe you can arrange to haul away the logs. By now, however, orchard owners have caught on to the fact that many people are burning wood. He may charge you, but his price is still likely to be lower than what you pay to a dealer.

Many Americans who own several acres of property in rural or semi-rural areas may have a woodlot (whether they know it or not). This is an area of land with a heavy growth of trees. In effect, it is a small tree farm. It can be managed in a way that will provide the owner with fuel for his own use or income from selling the wood to others, or both.

If you own such property or think you'd like to buy a woodlot and grow your own fuel, there are a number of publications available that will show you how it is done. See the Bibliography for a listing of these books and pamphlets.

Firewood Properties

The following hardwoods are listed according to the amount of heat they provide. Output depends on several factors, including the efficiency of your stove, the condition of your flue, and whether or not the wood is properly seasoned.

Tamarack is the only softwood acceptable for use as fuel. Its heat value is about equal to that of red maple. Other softwoods, such as pine, fir, and spruce, are suitable only as kindling.

Elm and sycamore are exceptionally difficult to split. Many veterans of wood stove heating won't touch them. But if you're faced with splitting elm and sycamore or being cold . . .

Wood	Splitability	Sparks	Smoke	Comments
Hickory, shagbark	Average to difficult	Light	Light	Among the heaviest of fuelwoods
Oak, red	Average	Light	Light	
Oak, white	Average to difficult	Light	Light	
Ironwood (hardhack)	Difficult; must be split while green	Light	Light	Repeat: Must be split while green
Apple	Difficult	Light	Light	Pleasant aroma
Beech	Average to difficult	Light	Light	Seasons best when split
Birch	Average	Moderate	Light	Split immediately to avoid decay
Maple Sugar	Average to difficult	Moderate	Light	
Ash	Average	Moderate	Light	Can be burned while green
Maple	Average	Light	Light	
Elm	Extremely difficult	Light	Moderate	
Sycamore	Extremely difficult	Light	Moderate	

Chapter 6:

You Own
All Those Logs
—Now What?

There it is, your cord of wood: a disorderly, formidable-looking pile of logs casually dumped in the backyard by the wood dealer's men who drove up in a truck, unloaded the wood, and left without a word of advice or consolation. Your wife is making remarks about the grass being ruined, and the kids have vanished, sensing there is work to be done.

Get busy. Now is the time to learn about sawing big logs into small logs, and small logs into splits that will burn well in your stove. Stack them properly so they'll season in time for winter use. Well, maybe you'll be able to con your wife and the kids into stacking them, the way Tom Sawyer did when he got his friends to whitewash the fence.

Sawing logs and splitting them isn't all that difficult a job. Besides, it's good exercise. As with any type of manual labor, the secret is in having the proper tools and knowing how to make *them* do most of the work instead of your muscles.

You may already own some of the tools you'll need, such as a chainsaw and a medium-sized axe. The items you'll need specifically for splitting logs are a maul, which looks like a cross between an axe and a sledge-hammer; a pair of wedges, which resemble axe heads; a chopping block; and maybe (but it isn't essential) a sawhorse. If you have cut down a tree on your property lately, the stump will do fine for a chopping block. One of your logs, cut to the right size, will also make a good block.

An eight-pound sledgehammer will handle about anything; six- or eight-pound wedges will do for all but the thickest logs.

As for the chainsaw, the amount of money you spend will depend on how much wood you'll be burning. You may already have a chainsaw. Fine, but is it strong enough to cut through a cord of wood, maybe more, without any strain? If you'll be using your stove only part of the time and won't need more than a cord of wood, one of the under-$100 saws should do the job. To play safe, however, you might be better off with a more powerful one, especially if you've got a cord of fine-burning hardwood out there in the yard. Hard-wood takes a heap of sawing. A weak chainsaw will have trouble and tire you out fast. Don't get a saw that's too heavy; that will tire you out, too.

If you've never used a chainsaw, or for that matter an axe, safety cannot be overstressed. Even the clothing you wear is important. Avoid shirts with flop-py sleeves and pants with wide bell bottoms. Sneakers and sandals are definitely out. Wear sturdy shoes or, better yet, outdoor boots of some kind. Gloves are es-sential. You'll be handling wood fresh from the forest— that means lots of splinters.

Also essential is protection for your head and face: eyes, teeth, even ears. Industrial earplugs or the type worn by swimmers are a good idea when you're using a chainsaw. It is noisy—plenty of decibels—and can do real damage to your hearing. Noise is also fatiguing.

Goggles will protect your eyes from sawdust and fly-ing wood chips when you're swinging that maul. A welder's or ironworker's shield will protect your en-tire face and won't fog up as quickly. Further protec-tion is available with a construction worker's hardhat.

If you're beginning to feel like you have to wear a suit of armor to saw and split those logs, remember that it's your head, ears, eyes, teeth, and other portions of your anatomy that need protection, especially if you're

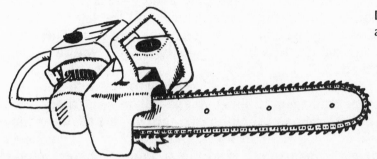

Don't strain or force the chainsaw; allow it to cut at its own pace.

new at this. You decide where to draw the line. Even a full suit of armor won't protect you if you're careless, but there's no reason why you have to suffer so much as a splinter if you recognize the potential for injury in using any tool—manual or power-operated—for any job.

As for using the chainsaw, follow the instruction manual. There are a few basic rules:

• Use the saw from the ground up. Start it while holding it on the ground, firmly resting there.

• Allow the saw to warm up for a short time to give the oil a chance to do its work.

• Go slow and easy. It doesn't take too long to get the feel of a chainsaw's action. Don't hurry things.

• Don't get overconfident. The majority of accidents with chainsaws occur among those who are most experienced with them.

• Don't strain or force the chainsaw; allow it to cut at its own pace. The work will go fast enough, and you won't damage the saw or yourself.

Cutting ordinary wood into firewood is called *bucking*. Begin by laying a log across a sawhorse or two other fairly equal-sized logs and cutting it to the proper length for your stove with your chainsaw. There is one main problem: once you've made your first cut partway through, the two segments of the log will close on the chain and stop the saw dead. This may damage the saw, can be dangerous, and slows down your work. To avoid this, make an *undercut* first, if the log is on a sawhorse, and then cut through from the top. If you're cutting with the log across two other logs on the ground, you won't have enough clearance to make an under-cut. Make the top cut first, then roll the log over and make another top cut. Before long, your muscles and your chainsaw will tell you how well you're doing things.

Now that you've cut all that big timber into smaller, more manageable logs, you've got to split them and then cut some of them into kindling. This requires the use of those other strange-looking implements you now own—an axe to cut kindling, a sledgehammer, maul, and wedges for splitting the logs. These procedures require even more caution than the use of the chainsaw.

Here again, protect your body from injury; beware of splinters, flying logs, a sharp axe or maul, and that heavy sledgehammer.

Place the log upright on the chopping block. If the log isn't very thick, all you'll need is the maul. Slowly swing the maul, aiming for the center of the log. Bend your knees enough so that the maul handle will be parallel to the ground when it has completed the stroke and split the log. In that way, if you should miscalculate and miss the log or the chopping block, the maul will strike the ground instead of your foot. You might practice striking the chopping block with several light blows until you get into the motion of the swing.

Go slowly, experiment. Don't start with the thickest logs. Splitting a few of the lighter ones with an axe might be smart if you're a complete novice at bucking wood. And don't strain with the maul. Let its weight do the work; that's why it's so heavy. Allow it almost to fall, using only enough muscle to guide it. The same holds true for the sledgehammer.

By now you're getting the hang of it, and that pile of big logs is getting smaller as the pile of smaller logs grows. You want to tackle the thicker logs. Your now-experienced eye tells you that the maul won't split this big one. Time for the wedge-and-sledge treatment.

Using the maul, cut a place at least a half-inch into the log for the wedge to fit, parallel to the grain. This is done with the wedge flat on the ground in front of you. Fit the wedge into the slot, tapping it in firmly with the sledgehammer. Now give the wedge a shot with the sledgehammer. Split the log? Good. No? Try again. If the log is very thick, or long, or over eighteen inches, you'll need two wedges, spaced accordingly. Try that.

Wedge-and-sledge splitting requires some experimentation by the novice.

Another way of splitting logs is similar to slicing pie. This works best with short, thick logs about twelve inches in length. Set the log on end atop the chopping block and make a cut so the axe or maul hits not in the center of the log, but a few inches inside from the bark. Make more cuts all around—like slicing a pie—until you've got several splits of firewood just right for burning.

This muscle-building (or fatigue-causing) work doesn't have to be completed in one afternoon. While you take breaks from happily sawing big logs into small logs, and then chopping those little logs into splits, the kids can be doing the stacking—under your close supervision, of course. Stacking firewood is considered a craft by old-timers who had to depend solely on properly seasoned wood to keep warm all winter.

The goal is to stack the wood in such a way that it dries within a reasonable period of time, and it doesn't come tumbling down and have to be restacked.

The proper way to stack your firewood depends on how wet it is. Wetter wood naturally needs more air, sunlight, and time to dry. It doesn't have to be bone dry, of course; wood is highly absorbent and doesn't dry out completely anyway. Certain types of wood absorb more moisture than others and hold it for longer periods of time. Wood that has been properly seasoned will still be twenty percent moisture, about the minimum to be expected, for example, in the Northeast climate, but it will burn very well.

Splits of wood will dry faster than solid logs, of course, and logs stacked criss-cross with plenty of air spaces between them will dry faster than wood stacked solidly.

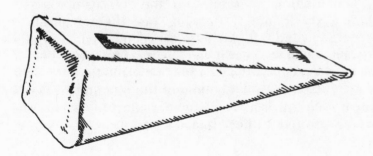

A wedge like this one is driven into larger logs with a sledgehammer.

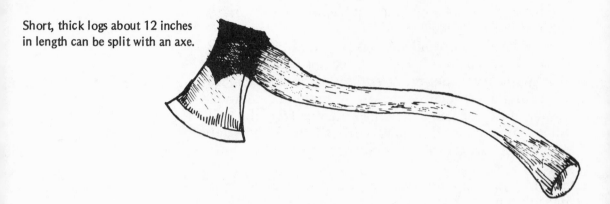

Short, thick logs about 12 inches in length can be split with an axe.

You'll have to test your wood to see just how wet or dry it is. Wet logs are heavier than drier logs. Wet logs will make a dull thud when struck together, while drier logs give off a sharp sound. There will be cracks and splits in the drier logs. In either case, you've got to stack and store your cord of wood properly.

First gather enough wood to fill your woodbox or whatever space you've set aside in the room where you have installed your stove. A child's large-sized toy box is a good place to store firewood for immediate use.

Your basic woodpile can be located anywhere with enough space where its weight—remember, firewood is heavy—won't do any structural damage.

A few good places to store wood are under the porch, on the porch, in the garage, in the cellar, or in a spare room of the house. Indoor storage will naturally accelerate the drying process since it is warm and dry inside.

Wood stored for too long will rot, and the heat-energy of the wood will be destroyed. Rotting is basically the same process as burning—wood breaks down into carbon dioxide and water which produces heat—but much slower.

The ideal temperature for the rotting process is about sixty to ninety degrees, just the temperature you'll have indoors during most of the year and outdoors much of the year if you live in a temperate part of the country. Check the woodpile now and then for signs of rot. It begins on the bottom of the pile and works its way up. Rotting is more likely to occur if the wood rests on the ground rather than on boards or a layer of bricks.

If indoor storage is impossible, the next best place to store wood is in a woodshed. In the good old days, no American home was without one, and your grandfather or your father (if he was a country boy) will recall that the woodshed was large, well-built, and used for many other things besides storing the winter's supply of firewood.

A woodshed for a moderate supply of firewood need not be elaborate. A lean-to structure is sufficient and simple enough to build of boards or galvanized iron sheets and a few two-by-fours. This will keep the rain out pretty well.

You may have seen wood piles covered with plastic or canvas tarpaulins. These covers are not only unattractive, they actually inhibit the seasoning process by preventing air circulation and keeping the sun's warmth from getting to the wood. Plastic, in particular, holds moisture in the wood. Rather than cover the woodpile directly with a plastic dropcloth or canvas tarpaulin, construct a tent-like structure to cover the top and part of the sides of the woodpile, leaving space between the top of the woodpile and the covering. This will afford some protection from rain and allow air to circulate.

Stack dry wood solidly, taking care that the pile is straight and steady, not leaning. You can stack the logs parallel, solid, in several smaller parallel stacks, or, as many woodpile experts recommend, in several criss-crossed stacks. Wet wood should be criss-crossed with lots of air space. However you stack firewood, brace the pile at both ends if it isn't in a woodshed or anyplace where there are no walls to keep it from collapsing. This is best done with a simple type of brace.

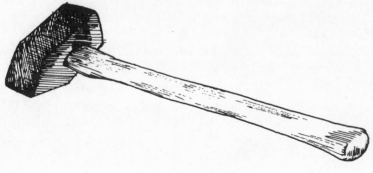

A maul is used to split medium-sized logs.

Tips on storing and stacking firewood:

• Store the wood as close to your house as possible, since you may be going out to get it in bad weather.

• If you store your wood against the house, stack it near a window if possible. Then you can hand the wood up to someone, or simply toss it in, for transport to the woodbox. This saves a lot of steps.

• If you've gotten a mixed cord of wood—more than one variety—stack it according to type so you won't have a slow-burning fire one minute and a fast-burning fire the next.

• Turn the wood every now and then, especially the top few rows.

• Work your way *across* the woodpile, not *down* through a stack, when getting a load for burning. The drier wood is on top and will give you a consistent, easier burn.

• Check the steadiness of the woodpile every so often, even if it's braced. Logs shrink and shift while drying.

Chapter 7:

Maintenance of Stoves, Chimneys, and Flues

The first maintenance chore you will face with your woodburning stove is the easiest one—emptying the ashes. In case you've forgotten, this is the grey substance that collects in the bottom of the stove. Figure that for every cord of wood you burn, you'll have about fifty pounds of ashes to clean out and discard. You will need the right tools to remove them.

If you have a stove with no grate (such as an airtight) you will need an ash rake. This is a thin metal rod with a rectangle of sheet metal attached to the end, resembling a garden hoe. If your stove has a grate, a small shovel (or something similar) made for the job will do the trick. You will also need a coal scuttle or pail to hold the ashes.

The rake, shovel, and pail should be metal. The rake or shovel should have a long handle so you don't have to place your hand near anything hot, and since there may be a live coal or two buried somewhere beneath the ashes, take all appropriate precautions.

You've cleaned out the stove, and there you stand with a scuttleful of grey ashes. What do you do with them? The simplest solution is to transfer the ashes to a paper or plastic bag and put them out with the garbage. Or take the bag to your local landfill, dump, or wherever. However, ashes can be useful. As long as you've come this far in the process of using a renewable resource, why cut off the cycle by wasting the end product?

Wood ash contains the minerals that were in the wood when you first slipped the logs into the fire. (The other components—carbohydrates and water—went up the chimney.) There are potash, calcium, potassium, magnesium, sodium, phosphorus, iron, silicon, and sulfur in the ash. Everything but vitamins.

All these substances are good for soil, particularly the potash if the soil is very acid. Sprinkle the ashes on your garden plot. They will give you better vegetables.

Besides sweetening and otherwise improving soil, ashes keep certain insects and other pests from getting at your plants. Slugs and snails, for reasons known only to slugs and snails, won't slither across ashes. It might be because the ashes are very dry and cling to their moist bodies and have some deleterious effect or other. Spread a layer of ashes around the soil at the base of plants you want to protect, and the little vandals will keep their distance.

An insect called the root maggot fly lays its eggs (larvae) on such vegetables as carrots, beets, and onions. These pests can be kept away by spreading a layer of wood ashes around the plants after they have grown six or eight inches in height.

Ashes can also be a physical barrier to insect pests. A shallow trench a few inches deep and a couple of inches across, filled with ashes, will protect tomato plants from cutworms. Young fruit trees can be protected from bark-borers by a layer of ashes around the base of the trees.

If you don't have a vegetable garden, there are other useful things to be done with ashes. They are at least as good as salt for melting snow. Ashes don't eat away the metal underside of a car the way salt does, and ashes won't leach into soil, as salt does, and possibly contaminate the water we drink. This is happening in many rural and suburban communities where environmentally ignorant officials authorize the spreading of large quantities of salt on the roads.

As for general maintenance of the stove itself, there

isn't much to do. A coat of stove-blacking once or twice a year will prevent rust and keep the stove looking good. Most of the maintenance with a cast iron stove is preventive: don't drop heavy objects onto it or bump into it since cast iron can crack.

Fires that become too hot can damage airtight stoves made with thinner-gauge sheet metal by what is called "burning through." The metal is oxidized away, causing thin spots in the stove walls. Although this is not likely to occur, check the walls of your stove before you light a fire.

If you have one of the enamelled stoves made by a Scandinavian company, be especially careful of a too-hot fire. Though the paint is exceptionally resistant to heat, with a tolerance of over 1,000 degrees, it has its limits. Follow the manufacturer's instruction manual as to its care, and you'll have nothing to be concerned about.

The airtights have door gaskets of asbestos rope. These wear out with time but are generally good for five to ten years before they need replacement. Occasional inspection of the gaskets is in order.

Your stovepipe will need more attention than your stove. Periodically inspect the pipe to make certain the sections are firmly connected. If the connections work loose and there are spaces between the joints, sparks and liquid creosote can escape, with obvious results. Elbow joints or bends of any sort are especially prone to working loose.

Any stovepipe will eventually corrode from the effects of such things as sulfuric acid (which forms from smoke condensation). The rate of corrosion depends on the gauge of the metal and how often the stove is used. Replace any section of stovepipe that even begins to look worn.

The major maintenance job is not with your stove or stovepipes but with your chimney flue. Chimney fires were discussed in detail in the chapter on safety. Avoiding chimney fires—and keeping your stove functioning efficiently and trouble-free—depends largely on a clean and safe chimney flue.

If you live in an older house with a masonry chimney that does not have a flue, it is essential that the chimney be inspected at least once each winter. Even assuming that such a chimney was in good condition when the stove was installed, the unusually harsh winters of recent years in the northeast and midwest have probably caused some abnormal deterioration of older chimneys. If the chimney has been in disuse or was used only to vent an oil burner, it must be checked and repaired before another winter of woodburning begins. A year's use of a woodburning stove, with all that unaccustomed smoke and heat passing through the chimney, may have been just enough to accelerate any deterioration.

If this is your first season with a wood stove, it is likely you've been doing something wrong: keeping your airtight stove in the closed mode most of the time, thus building up creosote, or burning wood that wasn't allowed to season thoroughly (creosote again). In any case, an occasional going-over of the chimney is sound practice.

For an older chimney, begin on the outside by inspecting the condition of the masonry. With the chimney acting as its own flue, the structure must be sound.

Start with the cap at the top of the chimney. If the cap is the slab type (a slab of masonry supported by four low columns) check for cracks, holes, and loose mortar. If the cap is the metal conical type or has a revolving ventilator of metal, lubricate the metal moving parts and check for looseness wherever the metal joins the chimney. Remove any rust with a wire brush and solvent; then coat the metal with rustproof paint.

Next inspect the flashing—the area where the chimney joins the roof. In older houses the flashing will most likely be made of lead; in newer houses it will be made of copper. If the flashing is in good condition, you won't be able to see what it is made of because it will be covered with tar. If the tar is torn or deteriorated, you may need not only new tar but new flashing.

If the cap and flashing are in good condition, check the chimney mortar next (if it is a brick chimney). With a screwdriver, gently probe for loose mortar between the bricks. Do chunks easily break away? If so, the chimney needs new mortar. If you're handy, you can do the work yourself. If a lot of mortar ends up on the ground beneath the chimney, a major repair job may be in order.

There is another way to determine the condition of

your chimney. It requires an assistant but takes less time than the screwdriver method and is more certain to reveal serious cracks in the chimney. Your assistant stays below with a piece of chalk (or anything that can make a mark on brick or masonry) while you go up onto the roof with a stack of wet newspapers or a laundry bag filled with damp rags. There must be a fire burning in your woodstove.

Use the newspapers or rag bag to stop up the chimney for a few minutes. Does smoke come through the chimney anywhere? Through cracks or small holes? If so, your assistant can mark the spots or point them out to you for marking. These cracks and holes must be repaired. You don't want air coming in through them— or, worse, sparks flying out and onto your roof.

If an older chimney without a flue is in serious condition, it may be worthwhile to build a new chimney or, at least, install a flue of ceramic material or steel inside in the old one. A flue-lined chimney is always safer and more durable than an unlined chimney.

If your house is fairly new, it will have a flue-lined chimney, and since flues last almost indefinitely, the only maintenance required is to keep it clean.

If the idea of cleaning your own chimney sounds formidable, have a professional do the job. There may be one in your area. Check the listing in the back of this book, or ask your stove dealer. With the resurgence of woodburning stoves, there has been a revival of the ancient art of chimney sweeping although the last time most of us even heard that term was in *Mary Poppins*.

You might want to give chimney sweeping a try yourself. It isn't all that difficult unless the chimney hasn't been cleaned in many years.

Professional chimney sweeps use a variety of brushes to remove soot and creosote. Most of the brushes have wire bristles in strange-looking shapes and sizes to fit various chimney flues. A century or so ago, chimney sweeps lowered small boys down the chimneys to do the cleaning—rough on the kids. Today's methods do a better job.

Do-it-yourself chimney sweeps use everything from Christmas trees to burlap sacks filled with rocks. You can obtain regulation chimney-sweep brushes from stove dealers and hardware stores. Amateurs who do their own sweeping say that a couple of tire chains attached to a strong rope, either in a burlap sack or un-covered, do a good job of chipping away at creosote (which is the primary problem in keeping a flue clean). You will also need a pair of heavy gloves and some-thing to protect your eyes and lungs.

Lower the chains to the bottom of the chimney on a rope of the appropriate length. Then haul the chains up, scraping away at the accumulated creosote and car-bon deposits. Cover all sides of the flue. You will find most of the deposits in the upper portion since the air is coldest toward the top. Cold air coming into contact with the hot smoke causes rapid condensation of the substances in the smoke.

Check now and then with your flashlight. Still lots of creosote? Keep scraping away until your arms are weary or the gunk is gone.

Are you wondering what happens to the chips of creosote that were scraped from the sides of the flue? Sure, they go down, but down to where?

Outside, at the bottom of the chimney, you'll find a metal door. You may have noticed it prior to installing your stove. It's called a clean-out door. Inside you'll find all the gunk that was stuck to the sides of the chimney. Clean it all out. What do you do with it? You can't spread it on your vegetable garden or use it to melt snow. Unfortunately, no one has thought of any commercial or home use for that creosote or carbon. You can only throw it out.

The chains-and-muscle method of cleaning your flue is dirty, somewhat dangerous, and physically de-manding if you aren't use to such work. If it's more than you care to handle, there is another way to clean the flue yourself—with chemicals. There are two schools of thought on the chemical method: one school says the method is of little use; the other says it works.

There are a number of commercial cleaning agents available. When sprinkled on a wood fire of the correct temperature, they send chemical fumes up the chimney that turn the creosote deposits to flakes. These flakes then fall into the fire and burn harmlessly due to a chemical reaction that changes their components.

The main ingredient of these commerical cleaners is sodium chloride—the same salt you sprinkle on your food. The manufacturers say that when used in the right amount with a hot enough fire, their products work very well. The U.S. Department of Agriculture disagrees, as do a number of woodstove experts. But these cleaners are worth a try if you want to avoid the job yourself and if there isn't a professional chimney sweep in your area.

Another method of cleaning creosote from a chimney is to deliberately set the creosote on fire. Many experienced stove owners do it, but chimney experts advise against it because it causes deterioration of masonry chimneys and can damage prefabricated ones. It seems strange that anyone would purposely set fire to his chimney when there are other cleaning methods available. I strongly advise against trying it—so strongly that I'm not even going to tell you how it is done.

Whether you clean the flue yourself or have it cleaned by a professional chimney sweep, you will have done the most important thing possible to insure your safety. Sleep easy.

Chapter 8

Woodburning Furnaces and Combination Furnaces

First came the fireplace, then the Franklin stove, then a proliferation of woodburning stoves. They were meant to heat an individual room or two rooms. But when we twentieth-century people think of central heating, we think not of wood fuel but of oil, gas, or electricity. Central heating with wood fuel? A woodburning furnace? Yes, and it can be as efficient as any other type of furnace.

As the energy crisis continues, more and more Americans are utilizing woodburning furnaces. They live in rural or semi-rural areas and are building new homes, or are renovating newly purchased older houses, or have been living in a home for some years and have junked their old gas or oil burners and switched to wood fuel.

All are concerned about being subject to the whims and problems of the oil companies and fuel dealers, the attendant price increases, and the real or calculated shortages of fuel.

Many people who had long been burning wood in stoves (perhaps a number of stoves in a large house) decided to convert to central heating and felt that wood

The Riteway No. 4 combination furnace is a basic wood or coal burner. An accessory oil or gas burner can be added. *Photo courtesy of Riteway Manufacturing Co.*

heat still made sense. They had been "into" wood fuel for so long, knew how to handle its problems, and saw no reason to convert to any other fuel.

Many woodburning furnace users are able to work both ends against the middle by installing a combination furnace. It can burn wood, oil, or gas, or by the use of accessories purchased later, can be converted to wood/oil or wood/gas. No matter what happens, these people will be able to get hold of some type of fuel.

Installing a woodburning furnace should be given much more thought than would be given to installing a woodburning stove in a living room. A furnace represents a long-term commitment and a major financial investment. It can't be thrown out, sold, or given away if you later find it doesn't suit your requirements.

The installation and safety rules that apply to woodburning stoves also hold with woodburning furnaces. The differences are that the furnace is much larger and more expensive than a stove and is kept in the cellar. Both its advantages and disadvantages are similar to those of stoves. You need a sound chimney flue and a place to obtain reasonably inexpensive wood that is good for fuel. You have to saw, chop, and split the wood, and the furnace isn't the type of heater that you glance at once or twice a year, leaving adjustments and repairs to the man who delivers your oil or gas.

It would be stretching the truth to state that a woodburning furnace has many distinct advantages over the average oil furnace. Even the most dedicated advocate of wood fuel isn't likely to argue that point very hard. Yes, the initial cost of a woodburning furnace is less than that of a comparably sized oil burner. Yes, wood is

The Longwood Dualfuel is a combination furnace which burns wood or, with optional equipment, oil or gas. The Dualfuel can also be adapted for use with central air conditioning. *Photo courtesy of Thermo-Control Wood Stoves.*

somewhat less expensive than oil, gas, or electricity. And yes, the trees aren't owned by huge corporations that seek phenomenally high profit margins and can manipulate the supply. But now you have to start hedging your bets.

The only fair way to consider woodburning furnaces is to avoid comparing them to other fuel burners and look at them as what they are: alternatives to other central-heating systems with certain intangible appeals that certain people find attractive for either practical or psychological reasons. These people may live in an area where wood is cheap and plentiful, or they may own a large woodlot. Others believe that wood is the fuel of the future and are planning ahead. A few are back-to-the-land advocates or dedicated ecologists. Whatever their reasons, burning wood makes sense to them.

Woodburning furnaces look pretty much like other furnaces—large metal boxes with a dial and lever or two. They work much the same as other furnaces: fuel them and set the thermostat, and they heat your house. They may be used in conjunction with any existing system that utilizes air, water, or steam for heating.

Unlike woodburning stoves, which radiate heat directly into the surrounding room areas, the woodburning furnace is enclosed by an insulated metal jacket that prevents most of its heat from escaping to the outside. Air entering the space between the jacket and the fire-box is heated and then passed through ducts to registers, radiators, or whatever.

Most woodburning furnaces are equipped with blowers that force the air upward and through the ducts. Others work on what is called the "gravity system," in which the naturally lighter hot air rises and passes through the ducts. Return registers in the rooms send cooler air back to the furnace where it is heated and passed through the ducts in a continuous cycle.

The blowers operate by electricity, and a number of blower-equipped furnaces can also operate by the gravity method in the event of a power failure.

Depending on its size, a woodburning furnace will run up to twenty-four hours without refueling. The combination types present no problem if you are going away for the weekend or are delayed getting home. When the wood runs low and the temperature drops

Thermo-Control's Model No. 500A functions either as a primary heat source by using existing ductwork, or as a back-up unit to an oil, gas, or electric hot-air furnace. *Photo courtesy of Thermo-Control Wood Stoves.*

Riteway's Model No. 2000 is an airtight stove. With an additional galvanized steel jacket, it functions as a furnace when ducted into an existing hot-air heating system. *Photo courtesy of Riteway Manufacturing Co.*

below your setting, the oil-burner portion of the furnace switches on automatically, so you don't come home to a frigid house, burst water pipes, and a frozen pet.

Woodburning furnaces used as a primary source of heat need plenty of wood to get through the winter. Many people in rural areas who choose to use them own property with an abundance of trees (a woodlot, perhaps) and spend many hours in healthful outdoor exercise—felling trees, trimming the branches from the trunk, sawing the tree into logs, cutting smaller logs, and stacking them in the woodshed or cellar. The latter part of this operation is important since there must be a ready supply of seasoned wood.

A sound chimney flue is vital to the safe, proper operation of a woodburning furnace. No alibis. A furnace is a *furnace*, not a small stove used to heat a room or two now and then. A furnace that is running constantly and burning a good deal of wood naturally causes more wear and tear on a flue. From the start, the flue must be in excellent condition.

One problem that isn't major with a woodburning furnace is creosote build-up. Furnaces are more efficient than most woodburning stoves. They burn the gases that often escape in less efficient woodburners to cause creosote deposits in the flue. Nevertheless, inspection and possible cleaning of the flue is mandatory once each season.

There are other factors to be considered when purchasing a woodburning furnace:

• Is there enough space in the cellar? Woodburning furnaces—especially the combination types—are somewhat larger than comparable furnaces that burn other fuels.

• Is there also space in the cellar for the large-sized logs that you'll be seasoning there? Furnaces take logs up to five feet in length. That saves you a lot of sawing and splitting, but you've got to have a place to put them.

• A woodburning furnace generates anywhere from three hundred to five hundred pounds of fine ash each season. Few backyard gardens need that much ash. If the ashes can be unloaded at the town dump or landfill, or the furnace owner has acres of land to spread them over, fine. Otherwise, you've got to get rid of them somehow.

Much of the above may seem negative, but "it ain't necessarily so," at least not to the people who have been using woodburning furnaces for many years. There are large areas of the country—very cold and remote areas—where nothing but wood is used to heat homes. When the blizzard is so fierce, the snow so deep, and the roads so icy that fuel-oil trucks can't make deliveries, the drawbacks of wood fuel are more than cancelled out by having a warm house.

A number of stove companies also manufacture furnaces while several companies produce only furnaces. Here are some of the dozen or so companies that manufacture woodburning furnaces:

• Riteway, which has been producing furnaces for about forty years, is unique in featuring a combustion chamber that can burn wood, coal, oil, or gas. The basic Riteway furnace burns either wood or coal; optional equipment is available that enables the furnace to burn oil, natural gas, or bottled gas.

• The Sam Daniels Company has been manufacturing its furnaces—called "chunk furnaces" because they can take very large, thick logs—for 65 years. They also

The Riteway Model No. 37 (similar to Model No. 2000) with steel jacket. *Photo courtesy of Riteway Manufacturing Co.*

produce wood/oil furnaces. All are old, well-proved designs with a rugged, no-frills look to them.

• Bellway furnaces are gravity-fed combination types. Logs are placed in a top section and ease down into the firebox as needed. This can be a distinct advantage if there isn't enough seasoned wood on hand. The wood dries while it is in the top section and is burnable by the time it is needed.

• The Newmac combination furnace is made by a Canadian firm and burns wood and oil in separate side-by-side combustion chambers. The woodburning section is based on the principle of the airtight stove. It is airtight and capable of burning wood with up to sixty percent efficiency. The ashes are so fine that emptying them is necessary only once or twice during the season.

• Thermo-Control furnaces can be used alone or in tandem with your present heating system and its existing fans and ducts. They can be equipped with optional interior pipes for heating water.

Chapter 9

Special Stoves
and Stove Accessories

Cooking Stoves

Mention a woodburning cooking stove or cookstove, and many Americans will recall the days in Mom's or Grandma's country kitchen back on the farm, the face-reddening heat of that big black cookstove, and the odor of fresh-baked apple pie or homemade bread. On farms today there are still many of these big, homey, country kitchens with a woodburning stove warming the family and baking those apple pies and loaves of bread.

Many of them are the same ones used a half-century ago; others are more modern versions that look different but work on the same principles as their ancient forebears. The woodburning kitchen stove must be included in the comeback of the woodburning heating stove.

According to the experts, Grandma's homemade bread, pies, cookies, and other delicious foods were so good because they were cooked on a woodburning kitchen stove. There may be some truth in that.

Whether the cookstove buyer is motivated by nostalgia or practicality, users of heating stoves are likely to have a woodburning stove in the kitchen, too. If it is a

Tirolia's *Thriftmaster* is the company's smallest cooking range, but it has all the features of their larger models. *Photo courtesy of "Old Country" Appliances.*

new stove, they can have nostalgia plus all the other benefits that come with burning wood.

The most up-to-date versions of woodburning kitchen ranges (most manufacturers call them ranges) are, at first glance, no different in appearance than the electric or gas ranges in millions of suburban homes and city apartments. They are available in white enamel or colors that fit the decor of any kitchen. They have doors, handles, thermostats—everything but the knobs that electric and gas ranges have. Woodburning ranges are available in many sizes, from huge multiuse models with turkey-size ovens to small models for use in bungalows and vacation cabins.

Old-fashioned stoves are still manufactured. They look exactly the same as those made a century or so ago; a few companies cast them from the original molds. They come in many sizes—from the huge farmhouse-kitchen model down to one that looks like a small potbelly stove with the upper half sliced off and replaced with a wide, flat top for pots and pans. A number of cooking ranges are able to burn wood and coal, and some companies make ranges that burn wood, coal, or oil.

The old-time stoves, to put it gently, were not marvels of efficiency. They were not airtight and thus devoured wood. They were large and required a huge firebox and spacious oven for Thanksgiving turkeys and such. Since they had to be opened to check on their tasty contents, wood was consumed rapidly as heat escaped. And since they didn't have thermostats, they had to be fussed with to keep a consistent temperature.

In winter the heating stoves rarely burned all night. Mom and Dad might take turns getting up early to go downstairs in the freezing house and light the kitchen stove while the kids waited until the fire was blazing and then raced downstairs to dress in front of its warmth. In summer the big cookstove was hell for mom. There was no other way to cook even when the temperature was in the 90s.

Modern ranges, however, are so well insulated that they give off no more excess heat than a gas range even with the oven going for hours. They are insulated with firebrick and equipped with thermostats for constant heat. A few of the larger models have hot-water coils, a

Tirolia's *Vienna* cooking range "cooks, bakes, heats your house. Hot water, too!" It burns wood, coal, and charcoal briquettes. *Photo courtesy of "Old Country" Appliances.*

great money-saver over electric or oil hot-water heating.

Among the manufacturers of a variety of kitchen ranges are Washington Stove Works, Birmingham Stove & Range Co., Tirolia (Austrian), Styria (also Austrian), Enterprise Foundry Co. (a Canadian manufacturer), and Stanley (Ireland). Until recently, the *Queen Atlantic*,—the grandmother of kitchen ranges—was made by the Portland Foundry Co. of Maine. But under new management, the company discontinued the Queen along with several other models.

Jøtul's No. 404 cookstove burns wood, coal, or coke; it roasts and bakes food and heats the kitchen. *Photo courtesy of Kristia Associates, exclusive importers of Jøtul stoves, Portland, Maine 04104.*

A combination cookstove and heater, the Jøtul No. 380 *Lumberjack* is designed for vacation cabins and hunting camps. *Photo courtesy of Kristia Associates, exclusive importers of Jøtul stoves, Portland, Maine 04104.*

Entire books have been written on the techniques and wonders of wood stove cooking, but good results, the experts agree, come from experience with a particular stove, just as a warm house depends on experience with a specific heating stove. Like a heating stove, a cookstove requires a certain amount of attention. You don't simply set a dial and go out for the day as you might do with a gas or electric range or a microwave oven. The cook does the cooking. This is a welcome change to many people who are fed up with instant, easy, simple, prefabricated, and frozen foods that are made in laboratories and taste like leftover leftovers.

Second-Hand Stoves

You've decided not to go all-out and buy a five-hundred-dollar airtight or an ornate Franklin stove. You'd just like to own an inexpensive, old-time wood-burning stove that will remind you of the days on your grandparents' farm, will look great in the living room or family room, and maybe even come in handy now and then. In addition old stoves can be worth money. Wouldn't it be great if you found a genuine antique stove in restorable condition? That would be like stumbling across a restorable Model A Ford or a mint-condition Edsel. Such things rarely happen these days. But you may pick up a fairly decent stove that could be worth restoring although it isn't likely to be an antique.

When buying any second-hand stove, the first thing to look for is cracks in the stove's body. You can't do much with a cracked cast iron stove short of having the entire section recast at a foundry. If the stove is a genuine antique and you plan to use it, the recasting will be worth the expense. But if you simply want it as an antique, not for heating, you can patch the crack with cement, smooth it down, and cover it with stove-blacking. Cemented cast iron will not withstand the heat of a fire.

If you run across a stove in otherwise good condition but with a part missing or badly damaged—a leg, door, or grate—you may be able to cannibalize the needed part from another stove of the same model or find an acceptable substitute from a similar type of stove. If your damaged stove is an antique and if the value warrants the expense, you can have the part recast.

After checking for cracked, broken, or missing parts, make sure the stove's wall isn't "burned out," that is, burned thin in any spots due to oxidation of the metal. This happens to stoves that have been used for many years or have been used to burn coal which burns at a higher temperature than wood. Pass by any such "burnt-out" case unless the stove is very rare, good to look at, and won't be used to keep you warm.

Rust is another thing to look for; lots of rust may mean that when you're through cleaning it off you'll have a thin firebox or a firebox with a hole in it. Clean rust and soot with a wire brush, steel wool, and solvent.

Many of the most valuable old stoves are ornate

parlor stoves with lots of brightwork decoration—
chrome or nickel "gingerbread," suitable for display in
middle-class or upper-middle-class parlors. Such
metalwork lasts for many years, and all it may take to
be restored is a light application of fine steel wool fol-
lowed by polish. If it is in bad condition, you may want
to have it replated. Again, cost factors enter the picture.

A number of flaws, more difficult to find, may be
present in an old stove: stripped threads where bolts
will have to go, patches of cement that have been

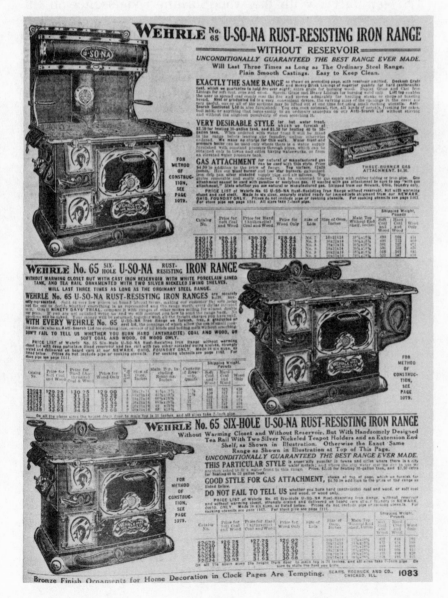

The Wehrle No. 65, from the 1911 Sears, Roebuck and Co. catalog, was available in three versions with various optional accessories. *Photo courtesy of Sears, Roebuck and Co.*

blacked-over. Make a thorough inspection of any old stove that you intend to use, not merely own for its intrinsic value.

Now that you know something about what to look for in an antique, classic, or older stove, where do you look? Many former users of woodburning stoves switched long ago to coal, oil, electric, or gas heating. And the faithful old hulk was carted out to the garage or barn or cellar (sentiment might not allow the family to part with it), covered with a canvas tarpaulin, and forgotten. One of them may be waiting for you, but better hurry. With the woodburning renaissance in full swing, the owners will be asking a premium price.

If you want to own an antique or classic stove but don't feel knowledgeable enough to buy a good one, or don't feel up to the hassle involved in the search, help is at hand. Dealers in old stoves are springing up here and there. Among them are Grampa's Stoves in Ware, Massachusetts, advertising "authentically restored classic and antique stoves," and Good Time Stove Company, of Williamsburg, Massachusetts, selling "authentic antiques in good working condition."

Do-It-Yourself Drum Stoves

Several stove companies sell drum (or barrel) stove kits—cast iron door, legs, flue outlet—for which you supply the drum and the work necessary to put together an inexpensive wood stove. They are also sold with the drum, assembled or disassembled.

If you want to try assembling one of the kits with your own oil drum (which costs only a few dollars), you only need some skill with a good power drill, a saber saw, and such ordinary hand tools as a wrench, screwdriver, and pliers. You cut holes in the drum for the door and flue outlet and drill holes for the bolts that fasten the door, flue outlet, and legs to the drum.

Your main problem may be with the drum itself because of its original contents: oil, solvents, pesticides, and such. The outside paint must be removed and the drum cleaned. How you clean the inside depends on what chemical had been there. You may have to use some kind of solvent to clean it or burn the chemical out. Cleaned drums are available from drum-cleaning

A small, open-ended barrel stove, the *Drummer* is available completely assembled from Washington Stove Works. *Photo courtesy of Washington Stove Works.*

A unique combination stove imported from Belgium, the *Efel* has a baffle system, cast iron-lined firebox and hood, and sliding glass doors. It is available in seven colors from Southport Stoves, Inc. *Photo courtesy of Southport Stoves, Inc.*

companies. They can be bought uncleaned for a few dollars from gas stations, junk dealers, and industrial plants. It isn't unlikely that you'll find one discarded in the woods or at the side of the road. In a country that abandons automobiles—literally throws them away— what's a mere steel drum? The drums come in a 55- gallon size, the most common, and in 15- and 30-gallon sizes.

What about the safety, efficiency, and convenience of a drum stove? See the chapter on safety; all rules apply. As to efficiency and convenience, the heat from a 55-gallon drum stove may drive you out of a cabin or bungalow but may be just right for a good-sized, uninsulated garage that has wide gaps in the door and windows. A drum stove isn't an airtight or Franklin stove, though.

The ready-made drum stoves claim to burn up to eighteen hours on a full load of logs. Maybe, but even if you cut that in half, it's good. If you make the cuts for the door and flue outlet carefully, fit the parts tightly, and don't expect miracles, you'll have a pretty fair stove.

Accessories

Woodburning stoves, like automobiles, can be adjusted to operate more efficiently and conveniently or have their appearance enhanced by the addition of various accessories—optional at extra cost, naturally. Most stove manufacturers produce such accessories for their own products; others are available from dealers. Among these are:

Heat reclaimers (also called *heat savers* and *heat extractors*): They come in two types. The passive type looks like a stovepipe with several rows of metal fins attached. The fins increase the area of metal surface available for heat to radiate into the room. Instead of passing straight up through the stovepipe and flue, heat is drawn to the fins' surfaces and passes into the air.

Active heat reclaimers operate electrically. They are box-like devices installed so that the stovepipe passes through them close to the top of the stove. In simple terms, air passes through a series of metal tubes inside the reclaimers, heats, and is then blown out into the room by a fan.

The *Culvert Queen*, a downdraft stove manufactured by The Stoveworks, is efficient and inexpensive. The corrugated firebox is about 10% greater in area than a flat surface of comparable size. *This material is published by permission of Lee Dora Gilchrist, Vice President, Southport Stoves, Inc.*

Both types increase the efficiency of a stove by providing more heat and thus saving fuel. The fins for the passive type may be bought separately and attach easily to the stovepipe.

Blowers: Operated electrically, blowers are used with circulating heaters to distribute air more widely, especially across colder floor areas.

Drum oven: This device is installed over a heating stove. It looks like a small drum-type stove set on end (there are also square models). It not only enables you to bake with a heating stove but also acts as a heat radiator.

Ash apron or ash catcher: A tray that fits beneath the door of the stove and prevents ashes—and maybe a hot coal or two—from falling onto the floor when you empty the stove. Many stoves are made with attached ash aprons.

Fire screen or spark guard: They fit across the front of the stove, usually a Franklin or combination stove, and prevent sparks from flying onto the floor and possibly burning down your house. A wise purchase to make.

Swing-out barbecue grill, cooking pot: Mounted to your Franklin stove on a bracket so you can cook. Use caution with these.

Brass knobs, brass rails: Good-looking decorations for Franklin and parlor stoves.

APPENDIXES

A Comparison Guide
to Woodburning Stoves

Prices are not included in this guide because of varying crating charges, freight fees from different parts of the country, and, of course, inflation. Prices would have been at best inaccurate, at worst misleading.

Manufacturers and dealers provide brochures and booklets with useful information on their products and wood heating in general. Many of them include price lists with their material.

American Airtights

Company & Brand Name	Construction	Features
All Nighter (4 models)	Steel, firebrick lining	Optional blower, hot water heating coils.
Birmingham Stove & Range Co.		
Nordic	Cast iron	Baffle system.
Ponderosa	Steel, firebrick lining	Baffle system.
Fisher Stoves, Inc. (3 models)	Cast iron	Secondary combustion chamber.
Hinckley Foundry (2 models)	Cast iron	Hand-crafted, based on 150-year-old Shaker design. Super-Heater model has heat exchanger.
Mohawk Industries *Tempwood* (2 models)	Steel	Downdraft system increases efficiency.
New Hampshire Wood Stoves, Inc. *Home Warmer* (2 models)	Steel	Side and rear baffle system.
Sevca Stove Works	Recycled gas tanks, steel	Heat exchanger; optional hot water coils.

Thermo-Control	Steel, firebrick lining	Downdraft system; can be adapted for use with existing heat systems.
Thermomatic (3 models)	Steel, firebrick lining	Downdraft system; bi-level top for extra radiation.
The Stoveworks *The Independence* (2 models)	Steel, reinforced with angle iron	Downdraft system; can be fitted with soapstone slabs to function as circulator.

Scandinavian Airtights

Jøtul (4 models)	Cast iron	Many features; contemporary designs.
Lange (3 models)	Cast iron	Larger models have heat exchangers.
Morsø (4 models)	Cast iron	Many features; contemporary designs.

Franklin Stoves

Atlanta Stove Works	Cast iron	Glass-paneled doors.
Birmingham Stove Works	Cast iron	Glass-paneled doors.
King Products Division Martin Industries	Cast iron	Can be used with gas.
Washington Stove Works *Olympic* (several models)	Cast iron	Doors fold against sides to save space.
Enterprise Foundry Co. *Old Colony* (2 models)	Cast iron	Doors fold against sides to save space.

Combination Airtight/Franklin Stoves

Efel	Steel, cast iron	Contemporary design; several colors; baffle system.
Fisher (2 models)	Steel, firebrick lining	Secondary combustion chambe
Jøtul (3 models)	Cast iron	Contemporary design; colors; doors slide out of sight when stove is in open mode.

Morsø (2 models)	Cast iron	Contemporary design; colors; baffle system. Doors fold back or lift off.
The Earth Stove	Steel, firebrick lining	Unique design; preheated secondary draft claimed to save fuel.
Vermont Castings	Cast iron	Secondary combustion chamber; largest flame path of any stove.

Circulating Stoves

Ashley (several models)	Cast iron, steel	Downdraft system; secondary air intake.
Atlanta Stove Works Homesteader (2 models)	Cast iron, steel	Lower front grille draws intake air from cold floor.
Birmingham Stove & Range Co. Knight (3 models)	Cast iron, steel	One model burns wood or coal.
Riteway (2 models)	Cast iron, steel	Can be converted to furnaces by adding jacket to existing duct system.
Shenandoah	Steel, cast iron	Available with or without jacket; will burn wood or coal.
Tirolia (3 models)	Steel, cast iron	Burns wood or coal; very compact.

Furnaces

Bellway	Steel	Logs gravity fed.
Longwood Dualfuel	Steel	Takes 5-foot logs; gas burners standard equipment.
Newmac	Steel	Works on airtight stove principle; 60% efficiency claimed.
Riteway (4 models)	Cast iron, steel	Combustion chamber will burn wood, coal, oil, gas.
Sam Daniels (several models)	Steel	Takes very large logs.

OTHER STOVES

Parlor stoves, potbelly stoves, box stoves, drum stoves, etc. are manufactured in a variety of models and sizes by many stove companies, including Washington Stove Works, Atlanta Stove Works, King Products Division of Martin Industries, Birmingham Stove & Range Co., Enterprise Foundry Company, and Edison Stove Works.

Parlor stoves and potbelly stoves especially have the old-time appearance we associate with woodburning stoves. Such stoves may not be as efficient as airtights, but they are nevertheless well-suited for use in homes and vacation cabins. They are generally less expensive than the airtights, Franklins, and circulators.

Manufacturers and Importers

The following list of manufacturers—who may sell through dealers or directly to the public—is necessarily incomplete due to space limitations. A manufacturer's inclusion does not imply a recommendation of that company's products by the author or Drake Publishers, Inc.

Abundant Life Farm
P.O. Box 63
Lochmere, New Hampshire 03252
Heating Stoves

Aeroheater Co.
P.O. Box 461
Springfield, Virginia 22151
Heating stoves

All Nighter Stove Works
80 Commerce Street
Glastonbury, Connecticut 06033
Heating stoves

American Stovolator
Rt. 7
Arlington, Vermont 05250
Fireplace stoves

Ashley Div. of Martin Industries
1604 17th Avenue
Sheffield, Alabama 35660
Circulating heaters

Atlanta Stove Works, Inc.
P.O. Box 5254
Atlanta, Georgia 30307
Heating stoves, ranges

Autocrat Corp.
New Athens, Illinois 62264
Heating stoves, ranges

Automatic Draft & Stove Co.
Lynchburg, Virginia 24500
Heating stoves

Bellway Mfg.
Grafton, Vermont 05146
Wood and wood/oil furnaces

Better 'n' Ben's
C&D Distributors
P.O. Box 766
Old Saybrook, Connecticut 06475
Fireplace stoves

Birmingham Stove & Range Co.
P.O. Box 2647
Birmingham, Alabama 35202
Heating stoves, ranges

Bow & Arrow Stove Co.
14 Arrow Street
Cambridge, Massachusetts 02138
Heating stoves, ranges

Damsite Dynamite Stove Co.
R.D. 3
Montpelier, Vermont 05602
Heating stoves, furnaces

Dawson Mfg. Co.
Box 2024
Enfield, Connecticut 06082
Heating stoves

The Earth Stove
General Engineering & Mfg. Co.
133 S. Snowden Street
Andrews, Indiana 46702
Heating stoves, fireplace stoves

Edison Stove Works
P.O. Box 493
Edison, New Jersey 08817
Heating stoves

Enterprise Foundry Co.
Sackville, B.C.
Canada E0A 3C0
Heating stoves, ranges

Fisher Stoves, Inc.
504 S. Main Street
Concord, New Hampshire 03301
Heating stoves

Franklin Fireplaces
1100 Waterway Boulevard
Indianapolis, Indiana 46202
Heating Stoves

Garden Way Research
P.O. Box 26W
Charlotte, Vermont 05445
Heating stoves

L.W. Gay Stove Works, Inc.
Marlboro, Vermont 05344
Heating stoves

Good Time Stove Co.
Rt. 9, Box 368
Williamsburg, Massachusetts 01096
Authentic antiques in good working condition

Grampa's Stoves
P.O. Box 492
Ware, Massachusetts 01082
Authentically restored classic and antique stoves

HDI Importers
Schoolhouse Farm
Etna, New York 03750
European-import heating stoves

Hinckley Foundry
13 Water Street
Newmarket, New Hampshire 03875
Heating stoves based on Shaker design

Home Fireplaces
Markham, Ontario, Canada L3R 1GE

971 Powell Avenue
Winnipeg, Manitoba, Canada R3H 0H4
Heating stoves, ranges, prefab fireplaces; Canadian
importers of Morso stoves

Hydraform Products Corp.
P.O. Box 2409
Rochester, New Hampshire 03867
Heating Stoves

Inglewood Stove Co.
Rt. 4
Woodstock, Vermont 05091
Heating stoves

Kickapoo Stove Works, LATD#
Rt. 1-A
LaFarge, Wisconsin 54639
Heating stoves

King Products Div. of Martin Industries
P.O. Box 730
Sheffield, Alabama 35660
Heating stoves, ranges

KNT Inc.
P.O. Box 25
Hayesville, Ohio 44838
Heating stoves, prefab fireplaces

Kristia Associates
P.O. Box 1118
Portland, Maine 04104
Heating stoves, ranges; exclusive importers of Jøtul
stoves

Locke Stove Co.
114 W. 11th Street
Kansas City, Missouri 64105
Heating stoves

Longwood Furnace Co.
Box 118
Gallatin, Missouri 64640
Wood/oil/gas furnaces

Maine Wood Heat Co.
R.D. 1, Box 38
Norridgewock, Maine 04957
Heating stoves

Malleable Iron Range Co.
715 N. Spring Street
Beaver Dam, Wisconsin 53916
Heating stoves, furnaces

Marathon Heater Co.
Box 165, R.D. 2
Marathon, New York 13803
Furnaces

Markade-Winnwood
Box 11382
Knoxville, Tennessee 37919
Heating stoves, furnaces, barrel stove kits

Merry Music Box
20 McKown
Boothbay Harbor, Maine 04538
Heating stoves, ranges; exclusive importers of Styria
stoves

Mohawk Industries, Inc.
173 Howland Avenue
Adams, Massachusetts 01220
Heating stoves

New Hampshire Wood Stoves, Inc.
P.O. Box 310, Fairgrounds Road
Plymouth, New Hampshire 03264
Heating stoves

Newmac Manufacturing Co.
Woodstock, Ontario, Canada N4S 7W5
Wood/oil furnaces

Old Country Appliances
P.O. Box 330
Vacaville, California 95688
Heating stoves, ranges; exclusive importers of Tirolia
stoves

Portland Stove Foundry
57 Kennebec Street
Portland, Maine 04104
Heating stoves

Ram & Forge
Brooks, Maine 04921
Heating stoves, furnaces

Riteway Manufacturing Co.
P.O. Box 6
Harrisburg, Virginia 22801
Heating stoves, wood/oil furnaces

Sam Daniels Co., Inc.
Box 868
Montpelier, Vermont 05404
Wood/oil furnaces

Scandinavian Stoves, Inc.
Box 72
Alstead, New Hampshire 03602
Heating stoves, ranges; exclusive importers of Lange
stoves

Shenandoah Manufacturing Co., Inc.
P.O. Box 869
Harrisonburg, Virginia 22801
Heating stoves

Southeastern Vermont Community Action (SEVCA)
7-9 Westminster Street
Bellows Falls, Vermont 05101
Heating stoves made from recycled propane gas tanks

Southport Stoves Div. of Howell Corp.
248 Tolland Street
East Hartford, Connecticut 06108
Heating stoves; exclusive importers of Morso stoves

Sunshine Stove Works
R.D. 1, Box 38
Norridgewock, Maine 04957
Heating stoves

Tekton Design Corp.
Conway, Massachusetts 01341
Wood/oil furnaces; exclusive importers of Tarm and
Tasso furnaces

Thermo-Control Wood Stoves
Box 640, Howe Caverns Road
Cobleskill, New York 12043
Heating stoves

Thermomatic
Rt. 145, Lawyersville Road
Cobleskill, New York 12043
Heating stoves

The Stoveworks
P.O. Box 172
Marlboro, Vermont 05344
Heating stoves

U.S. Stove Co.
P.O. Box 151
South Pittsburg, Tennessee 37380
Heating stoves

Vermont Castings, Inc.
Box 126, Prince Street
Randolph, Vermont 05060
Heating stoves

Vermont Iron Stove Works, Inc.
The Bobbin Mill
Warren, Vermont 05674
Heating stoves

Vermont Woodstove Co.
307 Elm Street
Bennington, Vermont 05201
Heating stoves

Washington Stove Works
P.O. Box 687, 3402 Smith Street
Everett, Washington 98201
Heating stoves, ranges

Weir Stove Co.
Taunton, Massachusetts 02780
Heating stoves

Whole Earth Access Co.
2466 Shattuck Avenue
Berkeley, California 94704
Heating stoves

Wilton's Stove Works
33 Danbury Road
Wilton, Connecticut 06807
Heating stoves, ranges

Woodburning Specialties
P.O. Box 5
N. Marshfield, Massachusetts 02059
Heating stoves, furnaces

Yankee Wood Stoves
Cross Street
Bennington, New Hampshire 03442
Assembled drum stoves

Chimney Sweeps

Following are members of the National Chimney Sweep Guild, a recently organized association. The author would like to thank Kristia Associates for making the list available.

Connecticut

AAA Chimney Cleaning, Saybrook
Tim Bobroske, Bristol
August West, Norwalk
Fred Toldo, Mystic

Georgia

Wood Heat, Inc., Columbus

Maine

Dave Brown, Bethel
Rod Cooke, Round Pond
Cliff Dixon, Yarmouth
Jason the Mason, Bass Harbor
Ron Mazzeo, Rockland
Mo-Jo's Chimney Cleaning, Westbrook
Bill Reynolds, Belfast
Dana Roberts, Kingfield
Al Sumner, Bethel

Massachusetts

John Arena, Natick
Stephen Brown, North Chatham
Bob Carlson, Glendale
Ken Hinkley, Williamsburg
Jeff Ludlow, Cohasset
The Work Collaborative, Amherst, Concord

Michigan

Don Davis, Gregory
Larry Hempsall, Grand Lake
Paul Nevermann, Dearborn

New Hampshire

Harold Higgins, Portsmouth
Jim George, Jackson

New Jersey

Mobile Chimney Clean, Midland
Bob Weiler, Egg Harbor

New York

R. Ernest Boice, Staatsburg
The Chimney Sweep Co. of Western N.Y.,
    Williamsburg
S & H Chimney Sweep Co., Portville

Pennsylvania

Will Hartzell, Kimberton
Landscape II, State College
Marcell Goodwin, Windber

Rhode Island

Philip Rondina, Middletown

Vermont

Bill's Clean Sweep, Williston
Black Magic Chimney Sweeps, Stowe
Chimney Care Products & Services, Cavendish
Green Mountain Chimney Sweep, Bennington

Appendix D

Catalogs

The Country Catalog
Frizelle-Enos Co., Inc.
265 Petaluma Avenue
Sebastopol, California 95472
$2.95; $2.50 refunded with first order of $20.00 or more.

A 144-page catalog, about half given over to wood-burning stoves and accessories, with discounts on several brands. Also hand tools, machine tools, farm equipment, unusual lamps, ice cream freezers and other country-style food preparation items, seeds, animal traps, weather vanes, and more—at discounts.

Country Stove and Shelter
The Exchange Building
270 Farmington Avenue
Farmington, Connecticut 06032
$1.00

A few heating stoves, ranges, and woodburning furnaces; accessories, country items, kerosene lamps, Swedish-made workbenches, American walnut toolboxes.

Cumberland General Store Wish & Want Book
Cumberland General Store
Route 3
Crossville, Tennessee 38555
$3.00

A 250-page nostalgia trip to the country of a century or so ago. Several major-brand stoves; accessories and hardware; "2,000 items for man and beast": fruit presses; kitchen supplies; livestock butchering gear; windmills for generating power; water pumps for wells;

145

tools; harnesses; and so on. You can also order custom-built, horse-drawn vehicles—buggies, buckboards, farm wagons, a surrey with the fringe on top, and if you're really serious about heading west, a Conestoga wagon.

Lite-Wood, Inc.
P.O. Box 267
Flanders, New Jersey 07836
Free

Stocks several woodburning stoves, accessories, and chimney-sweeping supplies. Also chainsaws, power and hand tools, a complete line of woodcutting tools—axes, mauls, wedges, cant hooks, hookaroons, manual and machine-driven logsplitters.

Sodbuster
Rt. 5, Stevens Gap
Crossville, Tennessee 38555
$4.00 for a year's subscription (12 issues).

Published by Glen-Bel's Country Store. Many country items from Glen-Bel's and other country merchandise, mail-order houses. Several stoves and stove accessories, tools, farm equipment, lamps, furniture, Boogertown pottery, country classified ads.

Glossary

airtight stove A cast iron or steel stove with a tight-fitting door and sealed or welded seams. Air can enter the stove only through a vent (draft regulator) in the door which is opened and closed either manually or by thermostat action. Thus burning is controlled. Airtight stoves are generally more efficient than other types of woodburning stoves.

baffles Metal plates in the firebox that enable a stove to retain volatiles (combustible gases) that burn and provide additional heat. Baffles also force heated air to travel a longer path to the flue outlet, enabling more heat to radiate from the stove.

box stove A square or rectangular stove, made in both airtight and non-airtight models.

bucking Cutting wood into logs of a length and thickness suitable for burning in a stove.

cast iron An alloy of iron, carbon, and silicon especially suitable for stoves because of its durability and heat-retaining qualities.

chimney connector A length of stovepipe that runs from the stove's flue outlet to the chimney.

circulating stove A stove with a firebrick-lined, inner firebox and an outer metal cabinet. Instead of radiating heat into the room, this stove circulates heated air by means of a blower fan.

combination furnace A furnace capable of burning wood in addition to any other combination of fuels, such as oil, coal, or gas, with or without additional accessories.

combination stove A woodburning stove able to function as an airtight, with the doors closed, or as a Franklin-type stove, with the doors open for viewing the fire.

controlled-burn stove See **airtight stove**.

147

cord
A stack of logs whose length, height, and width total 128 cubic feet. A cord usually contains logs of four-foot length stacked to four feet in height and eight feet in length.

creosote
The substance formed when hot smoke vapors come in contact with a cold chimney flue. The creosote is deposited in the flue as a sticky liquid which hardens to a tar-like consistency. Burning of unseasoned (damp) wood causes abnormal build-up of creosote.

cull wood
Waste wood — twigs, small branches, roots, bark, sawdust — from logging operations, unsuitable for use as fuel.

damper
A metal valve or plate that regulates the flow of air (draft) into a stove.

downdraft system
The term applied to a baffle system in several makes of stoves. The air flow is directed down and then up behind a vertically placed baffle plate at the rear of the stove's firebox.

draft
The flow of air into a stove; one of the factors determining the rate of wood combustion and thus the efficiency of a stove.

drum or barrel stove
An inexpensive stove constructed from a new or second-hand oil drum and a bolt-on kit — cast iron door, legs, and flue outlet. Drum stoves are also available in assembled form.

efficiency
A stove's ability to produce the maximum amount of heat with the minimum amount of fuel. The most efficient woodburning stove will utilize 50 to 60 percent of the inherent heat energy in the wood.

firebox
The body of a wood stove.

firebrick
A clay insulating material used in many steel wood stoves to hold a hotter fire and protect the stove's walls and floor.

fireplace stove
An airtight stove that is vented through a heavy-gauge metal sheet which covers and seals the face of the fireplace.

flue
The inner lining of a chimney which protects the chimney structure from deterioration caused by creosote, carbon deposits, heat, etc. A flue is usually made of a ceramic material; insulated steel is used in prefabricated flues.

Franklin stove	A type of stove manufactured by several companies. It is named for Benjamin Franklin, who invented its predecessor, the Pennsylvanian Fire-place. The modern Franklin stove is made of cast iron and has two doors in front which may be closed or left open while the fire is burning. The stove heats more efficiently with the doors closed.
front-end combustion	By the use of a baffle, logs in several types of airtight stoves burn from front to back, as a cigarette burns. Such front-end combustion maintains an even temperature.
green wood	Unseasoned (damp) wood, not yet ready for burning in most wood stoves.
hardwood	Dense, heavy wood that is the most suitable type for fuel; it burns longer, steadier, and with much less (or no) sparking than softwood.
heat exchanger	A chamber on top of the stove's main portion which acts as a secondary heat radiator.
heat reclaimer	Metal fins or a box containing pipes and a blower fan which are installed around a stovepipe to collect heat and radiate it (fins) or circulate it (box) into the room.
kindling	Thin sticks of wood used to start a fire.
maul	A heavy metal wedge used to split thick logs.
parlor stove	An old-fashioned stove popular in Victorian times, often ornately decorated. It functions similarly to a Franklin stove and is still manufactured.
potbelly stove	Seen decades ago in railroad stations and country stores, the potbelly is taller than most other stoves, thus allowing more thorough burning of volatiles. Its small firebox requires short-length logs.
seasoning	The drying of logs intended for use as fuel.

softwood   Lightweight wood which burns rapidly and throws off sparks; it is not suitable for wood stove fuel except as kindling.

stovepipe   A thin-gauge metal pipe through which smoke and unburned volatiles pass from the stove to the chimney flue.

thimble   An air-ventilated cylinder of metal or fire-clay that fits over the end of a stovepipe and through the wall to the flue, providing protection against combustion of wooden wall laths and beams.

volatiles   Gases released during the burning of wood.

woodlot   Land on which trees suitable for fuel may be harvested for sale or use by the landowner.

Bibliography

Books

Gay, Larry. *The Complete Book of Heating with Wood.* Charlotte, Vermont: Garden Way Publishing Co., 1973.

Harrington, Geri. *The Wood Burning Stove Book.* New York: Collier Books, 1977.

Havens, David. *The Woodburners Handbook.* Brunswick, Maine: Harpswell Press, 1975.

Shelton, John W. *The Wood Burner's Encyclopedia.* Waitsfield, Vermont: Vermont Crossroads Press, 1976.

Sherman, Steve. *The Wood Stove and Fireplace Book.* Harrisburg, Pennsylvania: Stackpole Books, 1976.

Vivian, John. *Wood Heat.* Emmaus, Pennsylvania: Rodale Press, Inc., 1976.

Wik, Ole. *Wood Stoves: How to Make and Use Them.* Anchorage: Alaska Northwest Publishing Co., 1977.

Magazine Articles

Abraham, George and Katy. "Wood Ashes Are Worth Money." *Organic Gardening and Farming*, January 1976.

Bacon, R. M. "Managing the Small Woodlot." *Yankee Magazine*, January 1974.

Casey, Paula. "Chimney Sweeps." *Vermont Life*, Winter 1976.

Cook, Sherman S. "Feedback on Stovepipe Power." *The Mother Earth News*, No. 24.

Country Journal's Guide to Buying the Woodstove That's Right for You. "Dealer's Choice." September 1977.

Dyer, Raymond A. "How to Build a Fireplace Fire." *Organic Gardening and Farming*, January 1976.

Fisher, Bonnie. "The Economics of a Wood Cookstove." *Organic Gardening and Farming*, October 1975.

Gay, Peter. "Chimneys." *Country Journal*, October 1976.

Gleason, Edmund. "An Old-Timer's Guide to Wood Splitting." *Country Journal*, October 1977.

Graves, Will. "Which Wood?" *Country Journal*, October 1977.

Hennessey, Madelyn. "The Woodpile." *Country Journal*, October 1977.

Jordan, C. J. and Cole, J. S. "The Shape of Things to Come." *Yankee Magazine*, January 1974.

Lyon, Jetta. "A Fireplace Is for Cooking." *Organic Gardening and Farming*, January 1976.

Manwell, Tom. "The Woodburning Furnace." *Country Journal*, October 1976.

Proulx, E. A. "Woodpile Axes." *Country Journal*, October 1977.

Shelton, John W. "An Analysis of Woodstove Performance." *Country Journal*, October 1976.

Smyser, Steve. "Making the Most of Your Woodstove." *Organic Gardening and Farming*, October 1975.

Stevens, Paul. "How to Heat a Large House with a Single Wood-burning Stove." *The Mother Earth News*, No. 35.

Stevens, Paul. "More About Chimney Fires." *The Mother Earth News*, No. 35.

Thomas, Dirk S. "Felling a Tree." *Country Journal*, October 1977.

Thomas, Dirk S. "How to Choose a Chainsaw." *Country Journal*, October 1977.

Vivian, John. "How to Cook with a Woodstove." *Country Journal*, February 1977.

Warner, Anne. "Tribute to an Old Friend." *Country Journal*, October 1976.

Wassil, Michael. "Stovepipe Power." *The Mother Earth News*, No. 24.

Wik, Ole. "How to Heat with Wood." *The Mother Earth News*, No. 48.

Wik, Ole. "How to Use Wood Stoves (And Use Them Safely!)" *The Mother Earth News*, No. 48.

Manufacturers' and Distributors' Publications

The Chimney Brush: The Homeowner's Resource Book on the Art of Sweeping Chimneys by Eva Horton, available for $2.00 from Kristia Associates, Box 1118, Portland, Maine 04104.

Morsø Wood Heat Handbook by Lee Gilchrist, available free from Southport Stoves, 248 Tolland Street, East Hartford, Connecticut 06108.

A Resource Book on the Art of Heating with Wood, available for $1.00 from Kristia Associates, Box 1118, Portland, Maine 04104.

Newspaper Articles

"What You Should Know About Wood Stoves." *Maine Times*, October 22, 1976.

"Woodstoves, 1977." *Maine Times*, September 23, 1977.

"Wood: An Old Flame Is Back." *New York Daily News*, January 26, 1978.

Publications on safety are available from:

National Fire Protection Association
470 Atlantic Avenue
Boston, Massachusetts 02210

A subscription to *Woodburners Quarterly* costs $4.95. Write to:

Woodburners Quarterly
8009 34th Avenue South
Minneapolis, Minnesota 55420

The U.S. Department of Agriculture issues a number of inexpensive booklets and pamphlets on woodburning stoves and wood fuel. Write to:

Superintendent of Documents
U.S. Government Printing Office
Washington, D.C. 20250

Index

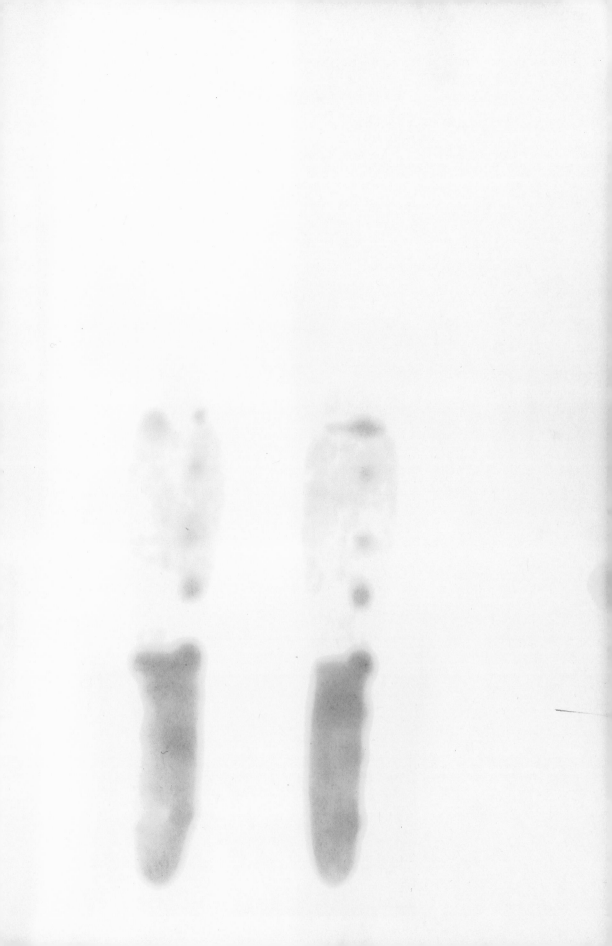